Playing Outdoors in the Early Years

Other Classmates:

2nd Series
Successful Subject Co-ordination – Christine Farmery
Parent Partnership in the Early Years – Damien Fitzgerald
Assemblies Made Easy – Victoria Kidwell
Homework – Victoria Kidwell
Getting Promoted – Tom Miller
ICT in the Early Years – Mark O'Hara
Creating Positive Classrooms – Mike Ollerton
Getting Organized – Angela Thody and Derek Bowden
Physical Development in the Early Years – Lynda Woodfield

1st Series
Lesson Planning – Graham Butt
Managing Your Classroom – Gererd Dixie
Teacher's Guide to Protecting Children – Janet Kay
Tips for Trips – Andy Leeder
Stress Busting – Michael Papworth
Every Minute Counts – Michael Papworth
Teaching Poetry – Fred Sedgwick
Running Your Tutor Group – Ian Startup
Involving Parents – Julian Stern
Marking and Assessment – Howard Tanner

Playing Outdoors in the Early Years

Ros Garrick

continuum
LONDON • NEW YORK

Continuum International Publishing Group

The Tower Building　　　　15 East 26th Street
11 York Road　　　　　　　New York
London SE1 7NX　　　　　　NY 10010

www.continuumbooks.com

British Library Cataloguing-in-Publication Data
A catalogue record for this book is available from the British Library.

ISBN: 978 0 8264 6872 7 (paperback)

Typeset by BookEns Ltd, Royston, Herts.
Printed and bound in Great Britain by Biddles Ltd, King's Lynn,
Norfolk

Contents

Preface   vii

Introduction   1

1 A Rationale for Outdoor Play in Early Childhood
   Education and Care   4
   Children's voices   4
   Can you remember?   5
   What are children's views?   7
   Changing landscapes   8
   Children's health   10
   An environment for learning   11
   Gender issues   13

2 The Place of the Garden in the Historical
   Development of Early Childhood Education   15
   Froebel   17
   Margaret McMillan   18
   Susan Isaacs   20
   The historical tradition of play   22

3 Perspectives on Young Children's Development
   and Outdoor Play   23
   Psychological perspectives   24
   Geographical perspectives: wild places   31
   Sociological perspectives: children's peer cultures   32

Contents

4   Outdoor Play Decisions   36
    Programme structure   37
    Unpredictable weather   40
    Messy play   43
    Gender   45
    Inclusion   51
    Health and safety   55

5   Planning an Outdoor Curriculum for Early
    Years Education and Care   60
    Curriculum frameworks   61
    The observation and planning cycle   64

6   Outdoor Learning in Early Years Curricula
    Internationally   87
    The Villetta pre-school in Reggio Emilia   87
    Forest Schools in Norway   89
    Growing Schools in England   91

7   Sources of Advice, Guidance and Support   94

References   97

Acknowledgements

I would like to thank those I have worked with in schools, early years settings and the advisory services in Leeds, Sheffield and Rotherham for sharing their practices and thinking about outdoor play. I would also like to thank colleagues at Sheffield Hallam University for their encouragement and constructive comments. Finally, I would like to thank my family for their support and good humour.

Preface

Playing Outdoors in the Early Years is for all those training to work with young children in early childhood education and care settings. It presents a rationale for outdoor play as an essential feature of the early childhood curriculum and explores how effective practice flows from an understanding of research perspectives. These include perspectives on children's development; perspectives on the role of adults in children's learning; and perspectives on the development of environments for play. This book identifies several challenging issues for practitioners raised by the outdoor curriculum. However, it also includes many examples of practice that exemplify the power of high-quality outdoor play and outdoor experiences to enhance the lives of children, their families and their communities.

Introduction

You can play in the secret house out there! Do you know how? Get some of those cardboard pieces you see around sometimes you know. Cover the ends of the tunnel with them and then play and do anything you want, even hide and seek! There are monsters and ghosts in the tunnel! (But just for fun.)
('Diana' Municipal Pre-school, 1990, p. 2)

The pioneers of early childhood education internationally, including Froebel, Issacs and McMillan, placed a special emphasis on the provision of outdoor play and learning environments for young children. Many contemporary practitioners, including those identified as exemplars of good practice, seek inspiration from this tradition and strive to promote high-quality outdoor learning. At the Diana pre-school, in the Italian town of Reggio Emilia, for example, five- and six-year-olds take pleasure in describing the fun of physical, imaginative and creative play in their school grounds to incoming three-year-olds ('Diana' Municipal Pre-school, 1990). In England, three- and four-year-olds at the Bridgewater College Early Excellence Centre experience the wildness of the natural world, exploring the nearby woodlands in all seasons (Grenier, 1999). As a further example, children at an American kindergarten (Perry, 2001) engage in exciting pretend play, supported by teachers who skilfully guide their social and emotional development. Each example evidences children engaged in rich, holistic learning experiences in outdoor environments.

There are many further examples of early years practitioners developing challenging experiential education for young children in outdoor settings. However, such practice is far from universal. Even where statutory guidance identifies outdoor play as an essential feature of the early childhood curriculum, (DfEE, 2000), differences in levels of provision are significant. In England, for example, 107 Early Excellence Centres provide models of good practice, with generously funded outdoor learning environments and outdoor space identified as a key quality indicator. However, some providers of nursery education have no outdoor provision and currently there is no requirement to develop outdoor areas as a condition of registration. Even where outdoor areas exist, use may be infrequent, the quality poor and opportunities for learning limited. A recent review of nursery education in the non-maintained sector in England and Wales (Ofsted, 2001) identified limited space in 10 per cent of settings, with a lack of large-scale play equipment and few opportunities for physical development. This deficit of provision suggests that the significance of outdoor play and learning is not universally recognized.

Ouvry (2000) examines reasons commonly given by practitioners for limited provision of outdoor play. The concerns highlighted include safety and staffing ratios, weather conditions, health issues, and the difficulties of access to outdoor space. This anecdotal list of concerns is supported by research findings from the Association of Teachers and Lecturers (ALT) (Ellis, 2002). ATL members in England and Wales were questioned about the implementation of the new foundation stage for children aged three to five. New statutory guidance includes a high focus on outdoor learning. However, 61 per cent of teachers working within the foundation stage identified the use of outdoor areas as problematic. A significant number of teachers reported a lack of management support for outdoor play and inadequate guidance for the development of outdoor learning environments. Such recurring contradictions between policy and practice suggest that outdoor play is very much a contested feature of early years education.

This book begins by examining the rationale for outdoor play in early childhood education and care. It moves on to consider the special place of the garden and outdoor experiences in the historical development of the sector. Following this, key theories that support an understanding of young children's development are examined, and the implications for learning and teaching outdoors considered. The next section examines some of the issues related to learning in outdoor environments. In subsequent sections, approaches to curriculum planning are discussed and examples of outdoor learning in early childhood curricula internationally introduced. The book concludes with information about organizations and agencies that can support the development of practice in this challenging area.

1

A Rationale for Outdoor Play in Early Childhood Education and Care

We need to be full of wonder at what children say and do, and hence curious to continue listening to and hearing what they say and do.

(Dahlberg *et al.*, 1999)

Children's voices

As the implications of recent international and national laws and conventions relating to children's rights are thought through, many policy-makers, researchers and practitioners are listening more attentively to children's voices. Internationally, the UN Convention on the Rights of the Child (1989) establishes an expectation that adults working with and for children should take account of children's distinctive perspectives, including those of the very young. Additionally, aspects of national legislation, for example the Children Act 1989 for England and Wales, reinforce this approach.

Thomas (2001) identifies three compelling arguments that underpin the recent emphasis on children's rights. When we as adults listen to children's voices, we are respecting the child's right to be heard; we enhance children's lives; and we can improve the quality of policies and practice.

For students and practitioners examining the rationale for outdoor play in the early years curriculum, this is a helpful approach. We need to attend to children's voices, as well as curriculum documents and official guidance. However, as adults we all too easily lose touch with the world as seen through children's eyes, even when working in close proximity to them. As we seek children's perspectives on outdoor play, personal memories can provide a powerful starting point.

Can you remember?

What were your favourite places as a young child?

A group of undergraduate students on an early childhood studies course were invited to reflect on five places they particularly liked and five they particularly disliked as children. The students and their tutor shared many happy and exciting memories. They also shared memories that evoked remembered feelings of anxiety, fear and, in many cases, unpleasant boredom.

It is salutary to note some of the disliked places and experiences common to even happy child-hoods. Many students recalled dreary, interminable shopping expeditions, with endless queues in shops, banks and at bus stops. Some recalled constraining visits to relatives, cooped up indoors with little to do. This reminds us that much of young children's lives is spent in adult worlds, tuned in to adult needs and desires that may not match their own. Less tangible but no less intense were the memories of fear and anxiety attached to dark and sometimes hidden places – under beds, on the landing or in a cellar. This reminds us that early childhood is a period of intense emotions of both positive and negative kinds.

Amongst the shared lists of favourite places, outdoor play spaces featured strongly. Many students recalled pleasurable experiences in parks and gardens. Mature students and their tutor shared additional memories of play beyond these domesticated confines. Memories dating back to the 1950s and 1960s were of wilder, more private places; for example fields, woods and streams, sometimes miles beyond the controlling gaze of adults. These recollections of wild places were rare amongst the younger students and this provides anecdotal support for the view that outdoor play experiences have become increasingly constrained for children in the economically rich, industrialized countries of the North.

There were clear differences across the generations but nearly everyone remembered at least one private and secret place that evoked powerful feelings of pleasure. Special places included a wild patch under fruit trees at the end of a long garden, a tiny space behind a garden shed and a spacious den hidden within tangled, overgrown bushes.

What are children's views?

Informal research with students highlights outdoor play as one of the most important and pleasurable experiences of childhood. Perhaps the adult's rose-tinted glasses play a part in creating such pleasurable images. However, more rigorous studies validate this view, providing detailed accounts of the outdoor places and experiences that are liked and disliked by children. Few studies focus primarily on the views of children under seven, but this age group is sometimes considered within wider studies.

Hart's (1979) important early study of children's outdoor play in a small US town was framed within geographical perspectives on childhood. Hart was interested in the ways that children used the immediate and wider outdoor environment of the town to play and socialize. As an ethnographic researcher, he lived as a member of the close community for two years, studying both the children's use of space and their personal feelings about place. An important finding was the importance that children attached to making special places of their own, the 'forts and houses' they regularly constructed in hidden places.

More recently, Millward and Whey (1997) studied children's play on English housing estates, seeking data to inform urban planning. Observations and interviews highlight children's enjoyment of both physically active play and quieter games. In particular, children value the opportunities to socialize and make choices afforded by diverse environments.

A methodologically innovative study (Clark and

Moss, 2001) examined very young children's perspectives on their experience of nursery, using, as one example, their own photographs of the setting. Findings highlight the special and positive feelings that young children sometimes have for what adults perceive to be very ordinary places. For Gary, aged three, a circular bench on a small piece of grass had the special properties of a magical cave, while a small piece of ground by the side of the shed was another important place.

These studies present strong voices from children, evidencing the importance of outdoor places and experiences in their lives. They also highlight the importance of finding ways to enable children to communicate their own perspectives on outdoor play. Children's views can concentrate our efforts to improve the effectiveness of outdoor provision. A number of other interlinking factors support arguments for an outdoor play curriculum. These will be discussed in the rest of this section.

Changing landscapes

Karen Miller (1989, p. 9) describes the sensual pleasures of outdoor play during a childhood lived on the edge of a Michigan lake, 'digging, sorting stones, finding snails, making mountains, rivers and dams, drawing pictures with a stick, dribbling mud and enjoying all the different textures at my fingertips'. She comments regretfully that contemporary children have diminished opportunities for such independent exploration of natural landscapes.

A Rationale for Outdoor Play in Early Childhood

Anecdotal observations such as this gain support from environmental sociologists, who study children's attitudes to the natural world. Nabhan (1994) reports that even children living in close proximity to nature have diminished first-hand experience of the natural world. Many Anglo, Hispanic and American-Indian children living in US country and desert areas are keenly interested in conservation issues. However, they now gain most information about plants, animals and landscapes from the media and school. These children are far less likely to explore their natural environments than previous generations. The experience of children in the city is bleaker still:

> ... an increasingly large proportion of inner-city children will never gain adequate access to unpeopled places, neither food producing field nor wild lands. They will grow up in a world where asphalt, concrete and plaster cover more ground than shade-providing shrubs and their resident songbirds.
>
> (Nabhan, 1994, p. 11)

The disappearance of opportunities for engagement with the natural world has significant implications for children's understanding of the environment and this is a real concern for early childhood educators.

Nevertheless, we should be wary of idealizing the childhood landscapes of the past. The history of early childhood education includes many educators who were committed to providing the experience of natural environments for children growing up in bleak and unhealthy cities (Bilton, 2002). Given commitment and imagination, practitioners today can similarly develop outdoor environments that nourish children's environmental understanding. This is an important part of the rationale for outdoor play.

Children's health

The impact of changing landscapes on lifestyles is just one factor contributing to increasing concerns for children's health at the beginning of the 21st century. Environmental change has limited the opportunities for children to engage in active outdoor play. This, combined with changes in diet and the increased use of technological-based leisure activities, has led to an epidemic of childhood obesity and related health problems across the developed world. Shell (2003) reports that between 1964 and 1999 the figures for childhood obesity in the US rose from 5 per cent to 14 per cent. There is a similar weight problem for one in five children growing up in Australia. In some countries of the rich North, a form of diabetes that usually appears in adulthood is appearing for the first time amongst overweight children.

Shell's (2003) review of research demonstrates the link between lifestyle and health. There are clear associations between the hours of television watched and children's risk of becoming over-weight or obese. Childhood asthma is another serious and growing health problem, again a negative consequence of changes in environments and technology (Robb, 2001).

A Rationale for Outdoor Play in Early Childhood

Attitudes to exercise and diet are shaped in early childhood, and education has an important role to play alongside national campaigns in reversing current trends. Pellegrini and Smith (1998, p. 592), reviewing research into children's physical activity play, argue for improved provision to promote children's 'health, in terms of cardiovascular and physical fitness'. Well-planned outdoor learning environments can significantly increase opportunities for children to engage in physically active play.

Unfortunately, it is those children who have health problems who are least likely to be confident in their physical skills. For these children, practitioners should note that positive, early physical experiences, for example the enjoyment of a 'Bear Hunt' obstacle course (Drake, 2001), can build confidence, self-esteem and positive dispositions. In addition, healthy snacks such as pieces of fruit and raw vegetables eaten picnic style in the outside area can reinforce messages about healthy lifestyles. A concern to take positive action, in the face of societal pressures undermining our children's health, is an important part of the rationale for outdoor play.

An environment for learning

Outdoor environments afford rich opportunities for physical learning. They also afford opportunities for other important experiences, not easily provided indoors. Baldock (2001), for example, suggests that the child's early experience of exploring large outdoor spaces may be critical to the development of spatial abilities. Curriculum guidance, such as that produced by The Early Childhood Mathematics Group (2001), recommends the use of outdoor environments to foster these abilities although underpinning research is limited (Baldock, 2001). However, Williams' (1994) study of nursery children's talk about play on a climbing frame evidences a child making significant progress in the use of language to explore concepts of speed, size and length over a six-month period of play outdoors.

Baldock also argues that outdoor spaces provide children with greater opportunities for independence than more adult-controlled indoor spaces. Evidence for this is again limited. However, Nind's (2001), action research study of language development in an early years unit suggests that young children may be relatively confident in their use of language outdoors because of their perceived independence from adult control.

Edgington (2002) also argues for the distinctive qualities of outdoor environments, suggesting that the outdoors allows for a valuable change of scale. This can be exemplified with reference to children's exploration of percussion instruments. Constraints on volume and space disappear outdoors. Children can enjoy a wider range of instruments or explore the sounds of large-scale percussion instruments. These and many more distinctive qualities of outdoor environments support the case for outdoor play.

Gender issues

Gender issues provide a final element of the rationale. The education of boys is a fiercely debated issue in many countries, including the UK and Australia (Yelland and Grieshaber, 1998). At the end of secondary schooling, girls are outperforming boys, and concern for boys' academic achievements is growing. In the UK, the government has identified an urgent need to 'challenge the laddish anti-learning culture' of secondary education (Henry, 2003, p.16). However, this response may come too late. In the UK, where an early start to formal learning is prevalent, some gender-related differences in achievement are evident by four and five years (Sharp, 1998).

It is useful to consider the evidence for early behavioural differences that may relate to approaches to learning and subsequent achievement. Despite some change in attitudes over recent decades, boys are often stereotyped as more aggressive, dominant, confident and active than girls (Schaffer, 1996). From this list of stereotypically male characteristics, Schaffer finds strongest research evidence for aggressive behaviour, with findings of higher levels of play fighting and rough-and-tumble play amongst boys. There are also findings of higher levels of activity amongst boys, although findings here are less consistent. It is important to note that because findings come from studies of large samples, there will be significant variation in levels of aggression and activity in any group of girls or boys.

Playing Outdoors in the Early Years

Given this evidence of early gender-related behavioural differences (Schaffer, 1996), early formal approaches may be more problematic for boys than girls, particularly in terms of dispositions for learning. Findings from several countries suggest a need to develop curricula that can more effectively nurture the learning dispositions of boys. An outdoor-play curriculum, offering opportunities for active play, exploration and the development of the language skills that underpin later academic development, may have an important part to play in boy-friendly early childhood curricula. Such programmes are likely to have more positive long-term outcomes than formal programmes for boys and girls (Sharp, 1998). This provides a final and significant strand in the rationale for outdoor play.

2

The Place of the Garden in the Historical Development of Early Childhood Education

How often in later life will their thoughts go back to the first garden, which, surely must be as rich as we can make it.
(McMillan in Bradford Education, 1995, p. 8)

There is a strong, contemporary case for the value of the outdoor curriculum in early childhood settings. Before looking to the details of implementation, it is helpful to examine two distinct strands within the historical development of outdoor play. The first strand is represented by the playground or yard of the elementary school tradition; the second is the garden of the nursery school tradition. The introductory discussion focuses on the UK.

From the end of the 19th century into the early years of the 20th century, many three- to five-year-olds attended elementary schools. Board of Education records for 1900 show that 43 per cent of this age group were in schools that offered poor, working-class women a cheap form of child-minding. Although children joined designated 'baby' classes, the system made no concession to their age or stage of development; group exercises in bleak school yards provided only limited relief from regimented learning in cramped and stuffy classrooms (Steedman, 1990).

The ideology of this tradition continued to exert an influence on UK infant and primary education into the 20th century. It has shaped a utilitarian view of the curriculum, a view that emphasizes the basic skills of literacy and numeracy, and a didactic approach to teaching (Anning, 1997). Many infant and primary schools, steeped in this tradition, have a similarly utilitarian view of outdoor play. Outdoor 'playtimes' are times for children to 'let off steam' between periods of 'work' of a mainly sedentary nature. Despite curriculum guidance relating to the youngest children in school (DfEE/QCA, 2000), this remains the typical pattern for five- to seven-year-olds, as well as for some four-year-olds. Many of these children play on featureless playgrounds or fields, with few play resources (Titman, 1994). Staffing norms provide only basic levels of adult supervision, with limited opportunities for adult–child interaction.

In contrast, from the early-19th century onwards, a tradition of nursery education shaped a very different approach to outdoor play across the US and Europe. There are significant differences in the ideologies and practice of key figures within this nursery tradition, as discussed below. However, there is an important continuity in the emphasis placed on the garden, and its identification as a special place for young children's play and learning.

Froebel

Froebel's educational practice and theories, developed during the first half of the nineteenth century, were influential in shaping the early history of the nursery garden. Growing up in Germany, and with a boyhood interest in nature, Froebel began work as an apprentice in forestry and later studied biology. His knowledge and intense love of nature, as well as a deeply spiritual approach to experience, informed an innovative approach to teaching. This was crystallized in his work with very young children in the later years of his life (Dudek, 2000).

The garden was at the centre of Froebel's educational work and in his first kindergarten it was a very real experience in children's lives. However, the term kindergarten also served as a metaphor for the nurture of the young and, for Froebel, symbolized an ideal social order. To encourage children to grow up in harmony with nature, Froebel gave each child their own small garden to tend. Individual and communal gardens provided flowers and vegetables, which were often given to neighbours of the school. Children were encouraged to observe plants and wildlife in the garden and were taken on excursions into the surrounding countryside. The key aim was to nurture children's spiritual awareness. Froebel's garden was also a place for exercise and play. He devised special songs and movement games for outdoor play, the forerunners of contemporary action rhymes and circle games (Hetherington, 2001).

Froebel's radical educational theories inspired many followers, initially in Germany but, in the following decades, across Europe, Japan and North America. Until the late 19th century, an expanding kindergarten movement remained faithful to Froebel's romantic ideals. However, the history of gardens within this tradition is a complex one and in the US, Froebel's spiritual ideals and practice were not sustained as kindergartens became integrated into the public school system (Hetherington, 2001).

In recent decades, some US architects have sought inspiration in Froebel's ideas and there has been a revived interest in the therapeutic value of gardens for children (Hetherington, 2001). Given children's diminishing levels of experience of nature and the high incidence of mental health problems in some communities, Froebel's focus on the garden as key to young children's spiritual development has continuing contemporary relevance.

Margaret McMillan

Margaret McMillan worked in England during the last decades of the 19th and the first decades of the 20th centuries and was influenced by Froebelian thinking. She had a diverse career in which children, in particular working-class children, provided a central focus for her work. Growing up in the US and Scotland, she was a prolific journalist, fiction writer, adult educator, socialist politician and social reformer. Her most significant achievements were founding a school medical service within an emergent welfare state and developing a nursery school in the slums of south London (Steedman, 1990).

The Place of the Garden

From 1884, working as an Independent Labour Party representative on a Bradford School Board, Margaret McMillan gained extensive experience of the harsh, unhealthy home and working lives of working-class children. She also gained experience of the bleak elementary school tradition that did little to ameliorate these lives. Following a move to London in the early 1900s, she pioneered a new children's clinic in Deptford, and it was here she came to understand the healing effects of outdoor environments and their potential for transforming young working-class lives. After running successful camp schools for older children, Margaret McMillan's interest turned to children under five. The Deptford nursery school grew out of the first open-air baby camp, and here Margaret McMillan developed her thinking about the nursery garden (Steedman, 1990).

Over two decades an extensive and beautiful garden was created for the children of this impoverished London community. The key elements were shelter provided by varied trees, bushes and terraced rock gardens; the sensory experiences of a herb garden; a vegetable garden providing food for the children's meals; cultivated and wild flower gardens; climbing equipment and sandpits; and a heap, for children to explore assorted natural and manufactured objects. The garden was designed to be on view to the community – to provide pleasure and an educational experience for parents as well as children (Bradford Education, 1995).

As a highly educated woman, Margaret McMillan was conversant with the most recent ideas about physical maturation, language development and stages in children's psychological development. The nursery garden was designed as an arena within which scientific and political ideas about childhood, in particular working-class childhood, might be explored (Steedman, 1990).

Margaret McMillan's work focused on children's physical and emotional wellbeing as prerequisites for intellectual development. This focus, as well as the contribution of the nursery garden to the lives of a community, has continuing relevance. The first State of London Children's Report (Hood, 2001) identifies significant numbers of children living in poverty today and confirms the continuing negative impact of poverty on children's health, including mental health. It remains important for practitioners to value outdoor environments for the part they play in promoting children's health and emotional wellbeing, as well as improving the quality of life for families and communities.

Susan Isaacs

Susan Isaacs is a third important figure in this tradition. Working in a very different social context, with highly advantaged children, Susan Isaacs opened the Malting House School in a large house in Cambridge in 1924. She was a trained infant teacher, as well as a qualified philosopher, psychologist and practising psychoanalyst. These distinctive perspectives contributed to the observations and analyses of children's learning that informed her teaching at the small, private school.

The Place of the Garden

By the end of three years at the school, Susan Isaacs had an extensive set of observations of children's play, investigations and thinking that were to provide the basis for three influential books about young children's learning (Drummond, 2000).

The children, aged between two and 10, had an unusual degree of freedom at the school, with opportunities to explore expansive indoor and outdoor environments. The garden was an essential part of the learning environment and some of Susan Isaac's most interesting and unusual writing focuses on children's experiences outdoors. The outdoor environment included areas that stimulated different kinds of thinking; spaces for bonfires; bricks in a building area; and an unusual seesaw that had moveable weights fastened underneath. At different times it included common, domestic pets and some more unusual ones, for example snakes, silkworms and salamanders. Alongside the animals, there were plants and fruit trees, providing a diverse natural environment (Drummond, 2000).

Susan Isaacs' writings evidence the ways that children's intense investigations and thinking about biological and spiritual concepts, including death, are supported by unconstrained experiences outdoors. Her writings, for example the account of children burying and digging up a dead pet rabbit, are likely to shock contemporary readers (Drummond, 2000). Nevertheless, Susan Isaacs' work has continuing relevance, and can support our understandings of the ways that vivid first-hand experience outdoors nourishes early cognitive and affective development.

The historical tradition of play

Discussion has focused on these three of many important figures in the history of early childhood education because their work represents three important strands in the history of outdoor play and the nursery garden. Froebel represents an insistence on the spiritual needs of the young child; Margaret McMillan represents an emphasis on children's physical health and emotional wellbeing; while Susan Isaacs represents a preoccupation with the young child's intense intellectual and emotional life.

The historical tradition of play has been invoked as an inspiration to contemporary early years practice (Bruce, 1997). However, Wood and Attfield (1996) warn against invoking this tradition uncritically in support of a play-based curriculum. They argue that, firstly, the tradition includes a mix of disparate and often contradictory ideas; secondly, the pioneers of nursery education developed their thinking in very different social and cultural contexts to those of today; and thirdly, the tradition cannot substitute for theoretical accounts of play and young children's learning.

There are, however, continuities as well as discontinuities in childhood experience, and it has been argued that the preoccupations of these three figures, Froebel, McMillan and Isaacs, have continuing relevance. In the section that follows, theoretical accounts of play and young children's learning will be discussed, supporting a deeper understanding of the educational role of outdoor play and experience in young children's lives.

3

Perspectives on Young Children's Development and Outdoor Play

Outdoor play settings may be the one place where children can independently orchestrate their own negotiations with the physical and social environment and gain the clarity of selfhood necessary to navigate later in life.

(Perry, 2001, p. 118)

Psychological perspectives, in particular the perspectives of developmental psychology, often dominate thinking about young children (James *et al.*, 1999). However, Raban *et al.* (2003) argue that acknowledgement of the complexity of children's development and learning suggests a need to consider the contribution made by multiple theoretical perspectives. They identify five psychological perspectives on children's learning that support practitioners in developing a range of 'practice styles'. In addition to these psychological perspectives, the intersecting and rich perspectives of sociology and geography are also important. The following section considers each of these perspectives on children's learning in outdoor environments, and the implications for practice.

Psychological perspectives

The growing and maturing child

Beginning with the philosophical writing of Jean-Jacques Rousseau (1712–78), the garden has provided a recurring metaphor for the nurturing of young children's natural growth within educational settings. Biological models similarly emphasize this early, natural unfolding of development (Raban *et al.*, 2003). Arnold Gesell and Mrtyle McGraw, who carried out extensive naturalistic observations of children in the 1920s and 1930s, charted children's physical development from early movement patterns to mature patterns of behaviour. Gesell extended this maturationalist thinking to cognitive development, again theorizing that children passed through a sequence of biologically determined stages. Such an exclusive focus on the biological programming of development is not widely accepted today. However, this early work was important in establishing child development as a significant area of study (Gallahue and Ozmun, 1998).

Today, a maturational perspective is often the commonsense approach of parents and educators, reflected in our language by such sayings as, 'She's just going through a phase.' This perspective suggests a mainly monitoring role for the adult during outdoor play, with development left to proceed at its own pace (Raban *et al.*, 2003).

This is a common approach to young children's physical development outdoors. However, Woodward and Yun (2001) argue that non-interventionist approaches may limit children's optimal development. In a study focused on the gross motor skills of young children in a US Headstart programme, they found that just over half the children had age-appropriate skills, while a significant minority were substantially delayed. The free-play programme, offering outdoor play but little or no adult interaction around physical skills, appeared to be ineffective in promoting the physical development of this group.

A maturational perspective may be satisfactory for some children. However, it may underestimate the adult role in nurturing children's dispositions to engage in physically active play outdoors through imaginative, varied and differentiated programmes of play and activities (Gallahue and Ozmun, 1998).

The pre-school child

Educators working within a readiness perspective emphasize the early years as a period of preparation for formal schooling; they construct the young child as a 'pre-school' child. Readiness perspectives grew out of biological models of development but placed a new emphasis on the role of experience in development. Informed by the behaviourist theories of the 1950s, the readiness perspective ascribes a more active role to the adult. This approach suggests that adults should firstly, identify deficits in children's experience that prevent readiness for formal learning and secondly, introduce activities to hasten readiness (Raban et al., 2003).

Direct instruction, implemented with sensitivity to children's interests and intentions, has an important part to play in early childhood settings (Siraj-Blatchford *et al.*, 2002). Outdoors, direct instruction is regularly used, for example, to teach circle games, to teach skills such as putting on jackets, and to give instructions for health and safety purposes.

However, the readiness perspective sits most easily within the elementary school tradition in relation to outdoor play. Here, adults provide 'letting off steam' breaks between longer periods of formal learning. This model is exemplified by the Miami pre-schools that were the focus of the Oxford Pre-school Research Project (Sylva *et al.*, 1980). Children in these centres engaged in short but intense periods of physical activity outdoors between longer periods of 'school readiness' activities. However, they demonstrated little of the intellectually challenging behaviour observed during outdoor play in the less structured Oxford pre-school centres. These findings highlight a potential difficulty with readiness perspectives. They may dichotomize physical and cognitive learning, and leave unrealized the opportunities for challenging learning across the curriculum outdoors.

The child explorer

Piaget's work, influential within early childhood education from the 1960s onwards, brings a very different perspective to thinking about learning and outdoor play. Piaget's innovative theory of cognitive development constructs the young child as an independent explorer, identifying the child, not the adult, as the person to direct learning. In this perspective, the adult role becomes one of guide; observing and assessing in relation to stages of development; then planning the physical and intellectual environment that will support children's active construction of knowledge and understanding (Raban *et al.*, 2003).

Piaget's work has influenced a number of early childhood education programmes, including an influential action-research study in an English nursery class (Athey, 1990). Athey worked as a teacher-researcher, implementing a programme to enhance the learning of inner-city children from severely disadvantaged families. The programme included an integrating focus on visits outside the nursery, including visits to a local park, to a local Police stable and boat trips on the Thames. The adult role in this programme involved work with families, to jointly observe and record commonalities in children's behaviour, identified as schema. It also involved finely tuned interactions with children, to support their development through different levels of cognitive functioning; from motor action, through symbolic functioning, to thought.

Outdoor play experience served an important role within this process, particularly at the level of motor action. For example, Athey (1990, p. 150) notes the children's fascination with spaces that contain and envelop and she describes how children first explored this schema:

> ... project observations consisted of children either putting objects into containers or getting inside enveloping spaces – climbing in

and out of enveloping spaces by various means, by steps and ladders, by crawling through, by levering themselves downwards into holes, and so on.

At this early stage of development, adults support children by maintaining a descriptive commentary on actions. Gradually, children take over the dialogue and begin to represent their experiences symbolically, for example through language, by drawing and painting, or through role play. Over time, action schemas develop into higher order concepts, often, as in the example below, supported by active outdoor experience:

Before Alistair (4: 6: 19) drew the tent ... and said that there wasn't enough room inside for more children, he had systematically explored the tent in order to extend the schema of envelopment ... His comments reveal a dawning awareness of the volume taken up by his own body in relation to the capacity of the tent.

(Athey, 1990, p. 154)

These examples suggest ways that adults, informed by cognitive developmental perspectives, can effectively support child explorers in outdoor learning environments.

The apprentice and friend

Although Piaget recognized the importance of the social and the affective dimensions of learning

Perspectives on Young Children's Development

(Siraj-Blatchford, 2002), this aspect was not the key focus of his theories. This contrasts with socio-constructivist perspectives that theorize children's learning as a social process. These perspectives, exemplified in the work of Bruner, Vygotsky and Brofenbrenner, emphasize the important learning that takes place in families and communities before formal school learning begins. Additionally, they bring to the foreground the essential role of the adult or more competent child, who provide leadership and guidance to the child through interaction (Raban *et al.*, 2003). Children learn in their roles as apprentice to adults and apprentice or friend with more competent peers.

Vygotsky and Bruner use the metaphor of scaffolding to explain how effective adult–child or peer interactions provide support for a child's learning, allowing the child to perform at a level beyond their independent capability, within their 'zone of proximal development'. The adult role is highly skilled, and it is one that parents may undertake more effortlessly than teachers (Siraj-Blatchford *et al.*, 2002).

The REPEY study of effective pedagogy in early childhood settings provides some examples of scaffolded learning, where skilled practitioners facilitate episodes of 'sustained shared thinking' around what are often child-initiated interests and themes (Siraj-Blatchford *et al.*, 2002). In one successful outdoor activity, practitioners talk with children over an extended period, as they closely observe and draw slugs and snails. The practitioners model language, extend children's vocabulary, and share their detailed knowledge of the animals.

Playing Outdoors in the Early Years

Where interaction of this quality occurs regularly, settings are particularly effective in promoting cognitive development. However, the REPEY study (Siraj-Blatchford *et al.*, 2002) highlights the low frequency of such episodes in most settings. Outdoor environments can provide rich stimuli to thinking and talk (Isaacs, 1932), but it seems there is a need for many settings to review the opportunities for adults to support episodes of 'sustained shared thinking' outdoors.

Diverse childhoods

A fifth perspective considered by Raban *et al.*, (2003) is that of critical theory. Critical social psychology places emphasis on the multiplicity of views of childhood and expectations of children that exist within society. It questions any notion of a 'normal' approach to working with children and challenges practitioners to review taken for granted practices within their own culture. This perspective questions the individualistic focus of psychology; it views children not as isolated beings, but as members of families and other groups within evolving communities. This approach suggests that the adult's role is to recognize children's relationships with diverse groups within the wider community, and to educate children in partnership with others (Raban *et al.*, 2003).

In thinking through the implications of this perspective for outdoor play, it seems important to engage families and the wider community in development work. Outdoor areas can be developed in partnership with community groups, and made available for wider use. Additionally, there may be individuals and groups with a special contribution to make outdoors, for example groups with artistic, craft or gardening skills. Exemplifying this approach, one London primary school, serving a culturally diverse community, collaborated with families to develop a very special garden. Families shared knowledge of plants from a wide range of countries of origin, contributing to an environment that could be enjoyed by all (Learning through Landscapes, 2003).

Geographical perspectives: wild places

Our sense of places that are special to us, in both positive and negative ways, is an essential part of who we are. This includes remembered places of childhood.

Geographical perspectives on children and childhood have focused on understanding children's developing sense of place. Several studies highlight the importance of wild places for children (Moore, 1985). For example, Nabhan (1994, p. 7), drawing on observations of his own children, identifies the important emotional experience of comfort and intimacy that children can find in nature. Describing his daughter's excitement at her den built under the low spread of a hackberry tree, he notes:

> Over time I've come to realize that a few intimate places mean more to my children,

and to others, than all the glorious panoramas I could ever show them. Because I sense their comfort there, their tiny hand-shaped shelter has come to epitomize true intimacy for me.

Trimble (1994, p. 24), reflecting on his own childhood, remembers the importance of natural objects, the collections of 'rocks, bugs, feathers, bones' that are the treasures of early childhood. He suggests that the experience of collecting enables children to develop a relationship with the earth, gaining a sense of security and worth.

Geographical perspectives have implications for the development of outdoor environments and play. They remind us that children need wild areas to support emotional wellbeing and nourish a relationship with nature. They also need time to explore, both alone and with peers, supported by adults who are sensitive to the value of independence and self-directed activity.

Sociological perspectives: children's peer cultures

Sociological perspectives also highlight the outdoors as a special place for young children's play, but emphasize the social purposes of play. Researchers identify outdoor areas as key physical and social spaces, within which children create their own peer cultures.

Corsaro (1997, p. 4) vividly describes a scene in the outside play area of an Italian pre-school where children enjoy their unique creation, 'a travelling bank':

> At some distance I saw three children marching around the yard carrying a large, red milk carton. ... There was a bucket inside the carton and it was filled with rocks.
>
> 'La barca?' I asked Antonio.
>
> 'No, la banca con soldi! (The bank with money!)' he said as he cupped his hand in a familiar Italian gesture.
>
> I was intrigued. These kids had created a whole new dimension in banking, a bank that makes house calls!

Discussing the episode, Corsaro explains how young children commonly draw on ideas and experiences from the adult world in play but often recreate these in unique and surprising ways.

As well as dealing with adult themes, children's peer cultures and play address their particular concerns as children. Drawing on observations of children playing in American and Italian pre-schools, Corsaro (1997, p. 118) suggests that children from three to six are intensely concerned with two themes. The first theme is that of social participation, for example establishing and sustaining shared play. Corsaro uses several examples of outdoor play to detail the strategies and rituals that young children use to enter and sustain shared play episodes. The second concern is with challenging and gaining control over adult authority, for example evading adult rules.

Perry's (2001) ethnographic study of yard play in an American nursery builds on the ideas of Corsaro.

Playing Outdoors in the Early Years

She examines the outdoor fantasy play of four- and five-year-olds and argues that spontaneous and child-directed fantasy play outdoors is significant for young children's social and emotional development. Children's collaborative learning is highlighted; children learn what it means to be a friend and how to take on the perspectives of others through the process of play. Although she identifies making friends as a natural process, Perry highlights an important role for the early years practitioner in supporting this. She documents the teachers' observations of the evolving peer cultures outdoors and explains how observations inform skilled and supportive interventions in play.

Connolly (1998) examines the social worlds of five- and six-year-olds, in a English, multi-ethnic, inner-city primary school. Although focused on the hidden curriculum of school playtime, rather than an explicit pre-school curriculum, this study has wider relevance and challenges practitioners to look more closely at issues of gender and racism in the lives of young children. Emphasizing young children's social competency, Connolly (1998, p. 2) explores 'the complex ways in which racism intervenes in young children's lives and comes to shape their gender identities within a peer culture. This important study (Connolly, 1998, p. 195) challenges 'traditional notions of childhood innocence' and offers support to practitioners as they develop multicultural and anti-racist strategies.

These studies highlight the complexity of children's peer cultures and the importance of themes of friendship, gender and ethnicity. They suggest a need for practitioners to observe very closely during outdoor play and, like Perry's (2001) skilled practitioners, use observations sensitively, to inform interventions that can promote social and emotional development.

This section has identified diverse theoretical perspectives on young children's development to inform practice around outdoor play. It has evidenced ways that outdoor play can enrich children's lives. However, there are recurring and often complex issues that arise for practitioners who aspire to develop outdoor play as an essential curriculum strand. Gender differences, for example, in children's use of outdoor play space present difficult issues, while balancing safety and challenge in outdoor play is a further concern. These and other issues will be considered in the section that follows.

4

Outdoor Play Decisions

> *... it is often through discussion with someone who holds a conflicting point of view, that we are able to clarify our thinking and reach new insights.*
>
> (Edgington, 1998, p. 201–2)

Practitioners who aim to work towards quality in outdoor provision have to make some important decisions about principles and practice. This section uses six outdoor stories to introduce key areas for discussion and decision making. The areas to be examined concern the relationship between the quality of outdoor play and programme structure; problems arising from adverse weather conditions; balancing the positive and negative aspects of messy play outdoors; resolving gender issues relating to space and styles of play; planning an inclusive outdoor learning environment; and meeting children's need for physical challenge. In exploring each of these areas, it is important to recognize that team members may hold diverse views. It is also important to acknowledge the diversity of early childhood settings; this militates against universal solutions to problems. Each staff team will need to explore the outdoor play issues independently, working towards shared viewpoints. In many settings, it will be important to access the perspectives of children, parents, carers and communities. This section presents research relevant to the issues raised and explores potential responses.

Programme structure

Outdoor story

Groups at Willow Nursery had a chance to play outdoors each day and today it was Ladybirds turn first. Reena watched and helped as her group of children rushed to be first with their coats and jackets.

It was a dull autumn day but the children were soon busily engaged outdoors. Several were keen to join the movement activity. Lively music accompanied them as they twisted and turned, making patterns in the air with brightly coloured streamers. Reena joined in the dance, praising and encouraging children as they moved. She also encouraged turn-taking, so that all children could enjoy the streamers.

Just one child, Maya, hung back. Maya stood very still, observing other children who played at the sand tray, built with wooden blocks and made chalk patterns on the ground. Her face was impassive and she did not move until the half-hour had ended. Reena announced that it was time to change groups and Maya's face brightened. She moved straight to the door and was first in the queue. She was keen to return to her home-corner play of the previous day. Amadur, however, was less enthusiastic. He had just filled his trolley with crates and was about to start transporting crates to the garage at the end of the path. This was not a good time to go in!

Later, at the weekly staff meeting, Reena shared her observations of Maya and Amadur. She felt that Maya was gaining little from outdoor sessions. Meanwhile, the battle to persuade Amadur to comply with coming in routines was exhausting for all. Reena was also concerned by Amadur's low-level play indoors, where he showed nothing of the concentration and persistence observed outside.

Reena's more experienced colleagues disagreed with her analysis. They argued that Maya had an entitlement to outdoor play, suggesting that any reluctance to play outdoors was normal for a new child and likely to be temporary. They were equally insistent that the programme structure was beneficial for Amadur, helping him conform to routines and take turns in his play.

The practitioner response: what would you do?

Some early childhood settings offer set periods of outdoor play, lasting from half an hour to an hour each session, providing each child with daily experience outdoors. During these periods, all children or a group play outdoors. Other settings provide opportunities for more extended periods of indoor and outdoor play, with children moving independently between indoor and outdoor provision. These are important differences in programme structure.

The Oxford Pre-school Research Project (Sylva *et al.*, 1980) compared the experiences of children in Oxford and Miami pre-schools and identified significant issues relating to programme structure. It seems that children who are free to begin and end activities independently, as in the Oxford pre-schools, are more likely to engage in the extended bouts of play that are associated with cognitive complexity. Amadur's transporting and garage play represents play of high cognitive challenge, as identified by the Oxford Pre-school Research Project (Sylva *et al.*, 1980). It is therefore important to consider whether a stop-start schedule that cuts across such play places limits on children's learning.

Laevers' (2000) research is also relevant to the issues raised. His 'experiential' approach to early education and care identifies young children's 'emotional wellbeing' and levels of 'involvement' as key indicators of quality. Laevers uses the term 'experiential' to identify a programme that focuses on the moment-by-moment experiences of the child. He argues that emotional wellbeing and involvement underpin deep-level learning and are key concepts for practitioners working to improve the quality of their practice. Inflexible structures may impede this process. For example, at this stage in her transition into the setting, group outdoor play was probably unhelpful for Maya. Adult support, encouraging co-operative play with new friends in the home corner, would have met her needs more effectively. In contrast, Amadur would have benefited, in terms of wellbeing and involvement, from adult support for ongoing play outdoors.

A final point concerns links between indoor and outdoor learning. Sylva *et al.* (1980, p. 60) suggest that play of high-cognitive challenge includes play that is 'cognitively complex, involving the combination of several elements, materials, actions or ideas'. Where practitioners encourage children to link indoor and outdoor themes and experiences, levels of cognitive challenge may be increased. A practitioner, supporting the play of Maya and new friends in the home corner, might suggest a picnic in the garden with the babies. This is one of many possibilities for linking indoor and outdoor play experiences. However, where fixed scheduling is in place, many opportunities for play that can help children to connect actions and ideas remain unrealized.

Unpredictable weather

Outdoor story

Gerrard was looking forward to his day outside. It was one of the real positives of the job that at least once a week he could work with children in the Mayville Nursery School's outdoor area. His enjoyment of outdoor play was one of the reasons that he had chosen to specialize in early years education at college.

The sky was blue as Gerrard and the team began setting up the attractive and diverse outdoor environment. The focus for the session was a mini-beast hunt. It had been planned after adults had observed the new children's fascination with worms, discovered in the digging patch a few days previously. Gerrard had organized resources to support the activity, with magnifiers, picture reference books and mark-making materials ready for use. However, by the time children had self-registered, the sky had changed. Black clouds threatened overhead and the air felt chill. Gerrard was unsure what to do but quickly decided that an optimistic stance was required. He checked that jackets were buttoned and zipped, and then gathered a group around him on the logs to see what he had in his special box. The children were enthralled as Gerrard introduced the menagerie of plastic spiders, beetles, caterpillars and bees. They joined in with his mini-beast rhymes, before enthusiastically taking up his challenge to set out on a real mini-beast hunt. The first group was a great success. At the end of the hunt, with raindrops beginning to fall, Gerrard encouraged several of the group to take the mark-making materials inside, to draw what they found.

However, as he gathered together a second group, the driving rain began. All thoughts of mini-beasts were put to one side as Gerrard set to work to bring necessary resources under the canopy or back into the shed. The rest of the day was a frustrating one for Gerrard and the children. The weather was changeable, a few more attempts at a mini-beast hunt were rained off and, by early afternoon, the grassy area was unpleasantly muddy.

Playing Outdoors in the Early Years

At the next staff meeting, Gerrard shared his frustration with the team. This led to heated discussion as to the value of planning for outdoor play when the weather was so unpredictable. One member of staff seriously questioned the value and appropriateness of persisting with outdoor play in unreliable weather.

The practitioner response: what would you do?

Where practitioners work in climates with fast-changing weather conditions, planning for outdoor play will need to be flexible. The weather can be frustratingly unpredictable for adults. However, most settings can expect hot, sunny days, wild, windy days and grey, rainy days on repeated occasions. Many settings will anticipate at least one bright, snowy day each year, while for others this may be a more regular occurrence. Children are likely to be excited by these events, as well as other surprising outdoor events. For example, where a garden includes giant, purple buddleias in flower, sightings of butterflies can be expected. The first sighting, however, will be a surprise. Events such as these are rich in potential for early scientific learning and practitioners should be well prepared to exploit them.

Children's understanding of scientific concepts is relatively undeveloped in the pre-school years. Keil (in Meadows, 1993), for example, discusses the case of a five-year-old who believed that rocks are alive. The child argued that rocks can have babies, evidenced in pebbles; rocks can grow, perhaps into larger rocks; and rocks can die, evidenced by their lack of movement. Meadows (1993) concludes that it is children's limited experience that is the key factor leading to errors of this kind. If incorrect conclusions arise from the limitations of children's experience, it is important that practitioners take advantage of all opportunities, including outdoor opportunities, to provide the first-hand experiences that feed conceptual development.

Responsive teaching in outdoor environments is most likely to happen where adults are well prepared to exploit exciting but unpredictable events. Ouvry (2000) and Edgington (2002) present ideas for planning that build on children's natural enthusiasm for windy and rainy weather, as well as other events in the natural world. If resources are well organized in advance, such plans can be implemented in response to daily events. In this way, a rainy day becomes not a problem but an opportunity for enjoyable learning.

Messy play

Outdoor story

It was a sunny spring afternoon and most of the children in the Brookfield Early Years Unit had chosen to play outdoors. Under the trees, a small group of girls had started to fill the shallow hollow of a tree stump, carrying soil by the handful from a nearby tractor tyre. With mounting excitement they collected twigs and sticks, added handfuls of mown grass and began to stir. Soon it was clear that this wasn't just a strange mixture on the improvised cooker, but a delicious 'chocolate cake'.

A younger boy, helping to fill the nearby water tray, came over with his bucket to see what was happening. He began to pour water slowly into the mixture, watching intently as it trickled onto the soil. The girls continued to poke and stir at the gooey and splattering chocolate cake but soon they were rushing off for fresh supplies. This time it was for 'sugar' from the dry sand tray on the other side of the playground.

At this point Kerry called to Miss Cohen to come and admire their cake. Miss Cohen was initially horrified to see the mud splattered on Kerry's t-shirt. Her mother would be furious. She was also aware that the cake was on the point of flowing out of the pan, onto the clothes of several other smartly dressed children. However, Miss Cohen also sensed the special qualities of the children's play and she was reluctant to cut across their intense pretend world.

The practitioner response: what would you do?

Child-directed play such as this rarely appears on adults' planning grids and can pose a range of problems. However, play of this kind may have a special quality of intensity, not found in more adult-directed play contexts. The special quality of play in this case arises firstly from the child-led social context, where children work with shared engagement and a high level of co-operation. De Hann and Singer (2001) highlight the significance of child-led play contexts for children's learning about togetherness and friendship. The intensity of the experience also arises from children's engagement with an outdoor place, incorporating a diversity of natural, open-ended materials. Children in this garden play with soil, twigs, grass, leaves, stones and sand, incorporating these into play themes. It seems that such diverse, natural places are particularly valued by children (Titman, 1994).

Exploratory and imaginative play in such diverse environments contributes positively to young children's development. However, there is a need for practitioners to plan for the manageability of such play. Practitioners who value this play need to establish appropriate dress codes for children and adults. Informal, easy-to-clean clothing and readily available aprons all contribute to the manageability of messy play. In many cases practitioners will need to share views about the importance of such play with parents, carers and, in some cases, school managers. In addition, children can be involved in discussing the issues that arise, perhaps outside the immediate play context. Children and adults together can develop rules to ensure the manageability of outdoor play. Children also need support to learn necessary practical and self-help skills, such as collecting and putting on aprons.

Gender

Outdoor story

It had been warm and sunny for two days, providing the first chance to play on the grass at Newlands nursery after weeks of rain. The grassy area by the apple tree had been set up with a climbing frame as well as tyres, crates, ropes and planks for building. A group of the older boys raced into the nursery garden as soon as the doors were pulled back and rushed past the home corner towards the building area. A saucepan was toppled from the cooker as they passed by and crashed to the ground. A small group of girls, who had settled to play at house under the veranda, called after them with indignant voices, 'You've spilt our dinner! We're telling Mrs Khan now, we're telling her!' There was no reply.

The boys rushed headlong into the construction area, cheerfully unaware of the upset caused. Soon they were engrossed in play, collecting and transporting crates for their quickly growing police station.

Mrs Khan had observed the incident and heard the upset voices. Seeing Ellie rushing over to tell the tale, she was inclined to suggest that the girls continue with their play and ignore this as just a minor incident. However, she was also aware that incidents of this kind were a daily occurrence during outdoor play. She was unsure what to do.

The practitioner response: what would you do?

It is important for practitioners to discuss the complex and sometimes puzzling gender issues that occur regularly during outdoor play in early childhood settings. Research from a range of theoretical perspectives can inform reflective practice.

Smith *et al.* (2003) outline psychological perspectives on gender that identify and theorize firstly, early sex differences in behaviour and secondly, developments in young children's own knowledge and understanding in this area. While boys and girls share many early interests, there is evidence of clear play preferences by the age of three and four, preferences of the kind observed by Mrs Khan. Girls tend to choose home-corner play, dressing up and playing with dolls. In contrast, boys are likely to enjoy more active play, for example block play, playing with balls, wheeled toys and rough-and-tumble play. By aged five, boys engage in more play fighting than girls, and they are more likely to behave aggressively. Smith *et al.* (2003) review cross-cultural studies which suggest that such differences in behaviour are relatively stable across cultures. However, there is some evidence of differences that relate to different societal expectations of girls and boys.

Alongside differences in play choices, young children also demonstrate a growing awareness of gender identity. Children are likely to show some understanding of stereotypically male and female play choices from two-and-a-half years. By four years, most children can identify their own gender and that of others, as well as recognize gender as a stable aspect of identity.

As Mrs Khan's experience suggests, gender is a salient feature of young children's identity and of their social worlds. To address the issues raised in practice, it seems important to seek explanations for these gendered behaviours. Some researchers emphasize 'nature' or the biological factors that may pre-programme behaviours from early childhood onwards (Smith *et al.*, 2003). In contrast, social-learning theorists emphasize the role of 'nurture', in particular adult reinforcement of what is seen to be gender-appropriate behaviour.

Cognitive-developmental theorists ascribe a more active role to children in the socialization process and explain the process of learning to be a girl or a boy as rooted in children's cognitive development. They argue that gender schemas, developing from early childhood onwards, serve to focus children's observations of peers, guiding their imitations of gendered behaviours.

However, a single explanation of gendered differences in behaviour may be too simple. Maccoby's (in Smith *et al.*, 2003) most recent research suggests that the development of early gendered behaviours is shaped by an interaction of biological, social learning and cognitive-developmental factors.

Cross-cultural studies evidence children's increasing preference for play and socialization with same-sex peers as they move through childhood (Smith *et al.*, 2003). Maccoby highlights differences in the behaviours of these peer groups, with competition and risk-taking characteristics of male groups, and collaboration characteristic of female groups. She argues that children's involvement in same-sex peer groups contributes positively to the development of sexual identity.

The implications of this research for practitioners are complex. At Newlands nursery, it may be important for children's development of sexual identities that practitioners support children's preferences for extended periods of play in same-sex groups. However, there may be problems in accepting uncritically the 'naturalness' of same-sex groups and gendered behaviours. Social-learning theory highlights a role for adults in shaping gendered behaviours and this raises questions about the values of the wider society in relation to gender and equal opportunities.

McNaughton (1992), working within the framework of feminist poststructuralist theory, highlights potentially problematic features of same-sex peer groups and gendered behaviours. She draws on research in Australian early childhood settings to argue that during free play boys regularly use physical power to control spaces, including girls' spaces. Although this seems to be part of learning what it means to be a boy, this kind of behaviour can have negative consequences for girls. The danger is that outside spaces come to be seen as boys' territory, while particular resources, such as wheeled toys, come to be seen as boys' toys. McNaughton suggests that practitioners should acknowledge gender as a category to support their observations of play. This is likely to lead to changes to the curriculum and to teaching styles. With increased awareness of gender issues, practitioners become, for example, more interventionist, establishing rules to support gender rights and challenging sexism during play.

In responding to the incident above, it would be important for Mrs Khan to reassure the girls that their concerns were recognized. It would be helpful to discuss the issues with the children involved, encouraging recognition of the need for boys and girls to respect the play spaces of others. However, rather than interrupting the flow of play, it might be more appropriate to plan for a reflective discussion away from the incident, perhaps during a small group or circle time. In a large-scale study of early childhood settings, Siraj-Blatchford *et al.* (2002, p. 12) found that effective settings developed strategies that 'supported children in being assertive, at the same time as rationalising and talking through their conflicts'.

McNaughton and Williams (1998) suggest that where practitioners introduce imaginative and human dimensions into play areas dominated by boys and where they model play, girls are likely to become enthusiastic players. In responding to the incident above, Mrs Khan would need to respect children's preferences for play in same-sex peer groups for some of their time outdoors. However, she could consider developing outdoor play themes with appeal to both groups, introducing, for example, a canteen in the police station. Information books could be used to promote further discussion about workplace roles and a widening of the roles children are confident to explore through play. Mrs Khan's active involvement in the play, perhaps in role as a police officer, could further encourage participation by the girls.

Finally, McNaughton and Williams advise that the process of changing gendered patterns of play is a complex one. Therefore, any strategies used will need to be monitored carefully for both intended and unintended consequences.

Inclusion

Outdoor story

Jonathan works at Montague House, an integrated children's centre that has a high proportion of children 'at risk' of special educational needs (SEN) in terms of low cognitive development and poor social behaviour. The centre includes a small number of children with statements relating to specific disabilities, including speech and language disorders and physical disabilities. Jonathan is a senior teacher in the centre, with special responsibility for children with SEN. He has recently taken on an additional responsibility for outdoor play and this has been identified by the staff team as an area for development.

The centre has three connected playrooms, opening onto a spacious paved area. There is a large grassy area, pathways for wheeled toys, a chequerboard garden and plentiful resources. However, to date the centre has focused little attention on the needs of children 'at risk' of SEN or children with disabilities during outdoor play. Jonathan sees this as the starting point for development.

The practitioner response: what would you do?

Jonathan has made a positive decision to focus on outdoor play to support children with disabilities and 'at risk' of SEN. A Learning Through Landscapes study of children and school grounds (Stoneham,

1996) presents clear findings of the value of school grounds for children with SEN. It highlights the importance of outdoor environments for the development of physical skills, for building confidence, and for promoting social and behavioural skills. A more recent study (Salmon *et al.*, 2003), focusing on children from three to six, highlights the importance of high-quality provision in improving the cognitive and social behavioural development of vulnerable children. Provision in this study was assessed using ECERS-R (Harms *et al.*, 1998), a rating scale that includes ratings of outdoor areas, as well as levels of adult supervision and interaction outdoors.

To develop outdoor play in this centre, Jonathan and his team should undertake a review of three key areas. They should consider adaptations and enhancements of the environment; the selection and arrangement of resources; and the quality of interactions during outdoor play, including adult–child and child–child interactions.

Doctoroff (2001), discussing indoor environments, provides useful suggestions for adaptations that can maximize the participation of children with disabilities in play. Jonathan's team will find it helpful to arrange defined play areas with visible barriers and to include some quiet zones, particularly for children who are over-stimulated by noisy play. In addition, pathways on paved areas could be marked and pathways on grass widened to ensure accessibility for any wheelchairs and walkers.

In selecting play materials, it is important to include resources matched to a diverse range of abilities across areas. For example, to promote motor skills it may be necessary to include three-wheeled scooters and pedal-less bikes amongst wheeled toys, while tactile and oval balls can be provided alongside traditional balls. Turning to role play, Dordoroff explains that children with cognitive delay are more likely to engage in pretend play if props, for example food and kitchen equipment, are highly realistic. However, non-realistic, open-ended materials should be provided for children who are more advanced cognitively. Where children have significant motor impairments, materials will need to be adapted and assistive technology used. A source of more detailed information is provided in the final section of this book.

The Montague House team should also consider involving children in the development of wildlife areas. Trees, shrubs, flowers and bird-feeding stations can be used to attract wildlife to the grounds. There is some evidence that such activities are particularly helpful for children with behavioural difficulties (Stoneham, 1997). The team could also develop sensory features within the garden, involving colour, light, texture, smell and sound (Bishop, 2001). Useful developments include a herb garden, an overgrown grassy area, mobiles, wind-chimes and the use of decorative tile or mirrored materials. Sensory experiences can contribute to cognitive and emotional development for a range of children (Stoneham, 1997).

Children with disabilities are likely to have delays in the area of social behavioural development (Doctoroff, 2001). Jonathan's team will need to provide resources to promote social play, for example balls, rocking toys, wagons, trolleys and tandem trikes. Outdoor role-play, for example a garage or shop, is particularly valuable.

Doctoroff suggests that clear organization of resources is important for children who have conditions such as Attention Deficit Hyperactivity Disorder (ADHD), where there may be difficulties in focusing and sustaining attention, as well as difficulties in regulating emotional responses. The Montague House team will need to ensure good organization and labelling of outdoor storage, for example using crates and shelving on wheels. Clear organization can help children to make play choices and to contribute to the maintenance of the environment. The placement of resources at appropriate heights is also important for children in wheelchairs. Where children have visual disabilities, it is essential to place resources consistently, and to provide warnings and additional help when necessary changes are made to the environment.

The quality of interactions during outdoor play is the third key area for review. The Early Years Transition and Special Educational Needs Project (Salmon *et al.*, 2003) demonstrates a significant link between the quality of adult–child interaction and the progress of 'at risk' young children, in terms of cognitive and behavioural development. The Montague House team could consider formalized evaluation and action planning to promote improvements in this area. Pascal and Bertram (1997) evidence the impact of the Effective Early Learning Project on levels of adult–child interaction in nursery settings, including interaction during outdoor play.

Peer interaction is a further area for review. Some studies (Hestenes and Carroll, 2000) evidence relatively high levels of solitary play amongst children with disabilities and relatively low levels of play with typically developing peers. Hestenes and Carroll suggest that practitioners need to be alert to the impact of organization and resources on interaction. They should also monitor the impact of their own interventions on inclusive play. For example, practitioners could observe the effects of assigning roles during outdoor role-play to promote co-operative play between the different groups of children.

Health and safety

Outdoor story

James was recently appointed as the team leader for the three- to five-year-old group in the High Trees Early Years Centre. In his previous setting, there had been clear and detailed health and safety guidelines for outdoor play that were followed by all staff. In this new centre, however, James was becoming increasingly concerned about the inconsistency of staff and the evident divergence of views in relation to health and safety.

A particular issue for the centre was the play of tall three- and four-year-olds. While most staff reinforced the agreed rule of 'up the steps and down the slide', Carole, a new member of staff, was allowing children to climb up the slide, slide down head first and even hang from the edge of the slide. When asked to reinforce centre rules by a senior member of staff, Carole had defended her approach. She argued that the outdoor play area was lacking in opportunities for physical challenge, particularly for older children. She also argued that the children were well aware of their own abilities and unlikely to take risks. James understood and accepted some of these arguments. Nevertheless, he was clear that his own responsibility for health and safety in the centre was paramount. The situation was complex and he was unsure as to how to proceed.

The practitioner response: what would you do?

Early childhood quality assurance schemes present a consensus on the need to promote health and safety during outdoor play. The Early Childhood Environmental Rating Scale–Revised (Harms *et al.*, 1998, p. 22), a tool used internationally for research and programme improvement, identifies 'adequate supervision to protect children's safety' as providing a minimal level of quality outdoors. At the excellent level of practice, 'play areas are arranged to avoid safety problems' and 'children generally follow safety rules'. Guidance of this kind is important to remind practitioners of their significant responsibility for children's health and safety. It is important, however, to acknowledge that such criteria may be deceptively straightforward. While we may all agree on the need to arrange play areas 'to avoid safety problems' (Harms *et al.*, 1998, p. 22), there may be less agreement concerning what counts as a problem.

Senda (1992), Japanese architect and designer of children's play environments, argues that contemporary societies have become overprotective of children in their concern for safety. As a consequence, children are increasingly deprived of physically challenging experiences, kept 'enclosed in a cage called safety' (Senda, 1992, p. 5). Senda's innovative play environments, including outdoor play structures for young children, are designed to provide opportunities for real physical challenge. Drawing on extensive observations of children's play, he argues that well-designed structures allow even young children to experience small dangers and learn how to deal with these. Stephenson's (2003) research in early childhood settings in New Zealand similarly highlights the importance for young children of physically challenging experiences – experiences that four-year-olds excitedly identify as 'scary'. She argues for a need to balance the positive features of risk-taking for young children with narrower discourses of risk in the wider society.

Senda identifies a common sequence of behaviours in children's use of play structures. At a first stage of functional play, children use the equipment as intended, for example climbing up the steps and sitting to go down the slide. After some experience, children move on to a stage of technical play. Now enjoyment comes from exploring new ways of using the structure and from mastering new physical skills. It seems that the children in James's centre are seeking novel and challenging experiences in just this way. Finally, at a third stage of social play, children begin to use play structures as settings for group play, for example games of tag or pretend play.

Most children seek novel and physically challenging experiences on play structures (Titman, 1994). Practitioners need to acknowledge this as an issue and discuss their response as a team. The provision of a safety surface under play structures is important and can increase opportunities for physical challenge. Good levels of staffing may also enable practitioners to provide appropriate levels of supervision for technical and social play.

Because permanent play structures can become unchallenging after repeated use, some practitioners reject them. It is also undesirable to have a large structure that dominates the outdoor area, limiting other play options. Titman, focusing on primary children, suggests that equipment for physical play should offer opportunities for change and manipulation by the children themselves. Stephenson (2003), working with nursery children, similarly highlights the value of movable equipment, for example tyres, crates, blocks, steps and planks. Provision of this kind allows children to participate in physically challenging experiences as they move equipment and design new structures. The environments created will be more diverse and offer greater novelty than most fixed structures. A-frames and ladders can be included to add variety and challenge.

However, if movable equipment replaces large-scale fixed structures, some valuable opportunities for physical challenge, for example swinging and climbing to a height, may be lost. The issues here remain complex. Each setting will need to find its own solution, achieving its own balance between safety and challenge in the physical play curriculum.

This section has explored some of the recurring and complex issues that arise for practitioners who strive to develop outdoor play as a key vehicle for young children's learning. Most teams will need to allocate time for observation and subsequent discussion to resolve such issues. Decisions will have implications for planning. There may be a need to adjust the long-term plans for a particular aspect of provision outdoors. Alternatively, changes may be required in day-to-day planning that informs practitioner's interactions with children during specific activities. Curriculum planning, as a valuable tool to support practitioners in promoting children's learning through outdoor play, is considered in the section that follows.

5

Planning an Outdoor Curriculum for Early Years Education and Care

> *The planning framework is a tool for the educator, not a straitjacket for children's learning.*
>
> (Rodger, 1999, p. 37)

Outdoor environments offer rich opportunities for learning and it is as important to plan for the learning that takes places outdoors as indoors (DfES/QCA, 2000). Planning as a team is particularly valuable. It promotes professional development, providing a context within which practitioners can share and analyse observations of children as learners, as well as ideas to support future learning. The conflicts that arise within teams, if sensitively handled, can initiate deeper levels of thinking about individual children and the outdoor curriculum.

Written plans should never limit the opportunities for learning that arise spontaneously and should be used flexibly. This is particularly important outdoors, where unpredictability is a feature. Daily planning, for example, can never predict children's excitement at the sudden appearance of a rainbow or a noisy helicopter overhead. Unpredictable events are often the most exciting and engaging events for children and many adults. Adults in the outdoor environment need to expect to be surprised.

Curriculum frameworks

The starting point for planning is thinking about the purposes or goals of early education. Purposes and goals are shaped by different cultures, and so vary across curriculum frameworks internationally (Spodek and Saracho, 1996). Because cognitive and affective learning are likely to be interrelated, planning will need to balance these aspects. However, the nature of this balance is a key focus of debate, with different emphases across curricula (Rogers, 1999).

The 'Experiential Education' project (Laevers, 2000), for example, places high emphasis on young children's emotional wellbeing and engagement with experience. It foregrounds the affective component of learning, with a focus on the goals of:

- emotional health
- curiosity and the exploratory drive
- expression and communication skills
- imagination and creativity
- the competence of self-organization
- understanding the world of objects and people.

Te Whariki (Ministry of Education, 1996), the early childhood curriculum guidance for New Zealand, similarly prioritizes affective learning with a focus on the principles of:

- empowerment
- holistic development

Playing Outdoors in the Early Years

- family and community
- relationships.

There is a similar emphasis in the curriculum strands that flow from these principles:

- wellbeing – *mana atua* (the health and wellbeing of the child are protected and nurtured)
- belonging – *mana whenua* (children and their families feel a sense of belonging)
- contribution – *mana reo* (opportunities for learning are equitable, and each child's contribution is valued)
- exploration – *mana aoturoa* (the child learns through active exploration of the environment).

In contrast, the curriculum guidance for English settings (DfEE/QCA, 2000) foregrounds children's cognitive learning, with learning goals organized within discrete curriculum areas:

- personal, social and emotional development
- communication, language and literacy
- mathematical development
- knowledge and understanding of the world
- physical development
- creative development.

Although this framework focuses on the affective component of learning with an emphasis on 'positive attitudes and dispositions' (DfEE/QCA, 2000, p. 8), the balance towards cognitive goals is greater than in some early years curricula. There is a significant overlap of purposes and goals of these three frameworks, despite the differences. The affective aspect of learning, for example, is common to all three but differently identified as emotional health, wellbeing and emotional development.

It is important to note that, even where a curriculum framework promotes thinking about learning goals within discrete curriculum areas, as in the English guidance (DfEE/QCA, 2000), much early learning flows over such boundaries. The holistic nature of young children's learning is appropriately highlighted by a range of guidance documents (Bredecamp, 1987). Many of the outdoor experiences most enjoyed by young children are rich in potential for cross-curricular learning. For example, children digging up potatoes in the garden are developing gross motor skills for digging; the scientific skills of observing and comparing; scientific knowledge and understanding of life processes; communication and language skills for talking; and a developing sense of emotional well-being. Extending the practical activity, a picture book about vegetables could be used to introduce early literacy skills; while children could represent and communicate experiences in the garden through the additional languages of collage, drawing and painting. With skilled and sensitive teaching, all aspects of this experience could be used to promote children's positive dispositions towards learning.

Each setting will need to make decisions about their approach to planning, informed by a range of factors. These will include national or more local curriculum frameworks and guidance; distinctive features of the setting, including the practitioner's shared philosophy; and the team's reflections on their own experience of working with children outdoors. The following section provides examples of planning an outdoor curriculum. The aim is to provide useful starting points for planning, but not to be prescriptive.

The observation and planning cycle

Despite the unpredictability of outdoor experience, the quality of children's learning outdoors is strongly related to the quality of planning. However, as Perry's (2001) study of outdoor role-play in an American kindergarten suggests, effective planning is not an isolated activity but part of a continuous cycle, closely linked to the observation, recording and analysis of children's learning. It is also a process that should be reviewed and evaluated at all stages. In planning an outdoor curriculum, it is helpful to consider planning at three different levels: long term, medium term and short term. The purposes of these different kinds of planning are discussed below.

Long-term planning of outdoor provision

The environment of an early years setting has been identified as a powerful tool for promoting play and development (Doctoroff, 2001). The range and quality of experiences offered impacts on the opportunities for learning. In addition, the organization of the environment impacts on behaviour (Aubrey *et al.*, 2000). Doctoroff 's review of research findings for indoor spaces suggests that complex play and increased levels of interaction between peers can be achieved by defining spaces with visible boundaries. The same principles apply to outdoor environments and suggest the advisability of zoning areas for specific kinds of play. Zoning can also impact positively on the way that children use and care for resources (Bilton, 2002). Fixed and aesthetically pleasing divisions of space can be used outdoors, for example, walls, seats, trellis and planting. To use the space more flexibly, changeable divisions can be improvized, for example, planted tubs, resource trolleys, crates and tyres.

The learning of children at very different stages of development and with different approaches to learning can be supported by developing outdoor areas, for example, a large construction area, as continuous or near-continuous provision. Open-ended resources such as construction materials can be used in different ways by children who are at different levels of knowledge, understanding and skills. The opportunities that are offered for children to repeat experiences are important and enable children to consolidate their learning. In particular the predictability of continuous provision enables children to plan their learning and to develop and extend ideas over time.

Long-term plans can be developed for specific areas of play provision. Linked to indoor plans, these highlight the ways that outdoor provision complements and extends indoor learning. For example, long-term plans for an indoor water tray could be linked to outdoor planning that allows children to explore the properties of water on a more expansive scale. Rather than simply duplicating indoor provision, it is important to think through the distinctive opportunities for learning outdoors.

Key areas of outdoor provision to include are:

♦ An area or areas for natural materials, including wet and dry sand, water and mud – additional materials can be provided at times, for example bark chippings, autumn leaves or shingle in a giant tractor tyre.

♦ A large construction area, including things like hollow blocks, crates, tyres and planks. Props such as a steering wheel, blankets, dolls and mark-making materials in a carry box, can be included to support imaginative play.

♦ A quiet area or areas duplicating indoor provision, such as small construction, books, jigsaws and mathematical apparatus.

♦ A creative area including painting and mark-making materials.

♦ A music area with percussion instruments.

♦ A den area – this could be an area for building dens with improvized materials such as a clothes horse, a variety of fabric and large pegs. It could also be a structure such as a small tent or collection of large cardboard boxes. A wild area can also offer hiding places.

- A large space for running and physical games like large ball games and tag.

- A garden area for growing flowers and vegetables. In small paved areas, plants can be grown in raised beds, hanging baskets, tubs and painted tyres.

- A small wild area at the edge of the garden to attract wildlife – this should include native trees, shrubs and flowers. In many gardens, a bird-feeding station, a log-pile and small pieces of carpet on the grass provide valuable additions.

- A physical play area, with climbing equipment on a safety surface. This can be made of loose pieces that can be assembled in different ways to offer variety such as tunnels, hidey cubes, steps, planks, A-frames, ladders and hoops.

- Role-play areas where children can imagine a garage and car wash or shop.

- A permanent or improvized roadway area with props including traffic signs, numbered parking bays and dressing-up clothes.

- An area for small apparatus such as balls, bats, hoops and a basketball hoop.

Areas can be provided on different scales, depending on budget and available space. For example, a crate with three small percussion instruments could serve as music area. Alternatively, giant-sized percussion instruments or musical mobiles could be provided as a permanent feature.

Playing Outdoors in the Early Years

It is important to ensure a balance of activities, with space for vigorous, active play, as well as space for quieter play. Some children may need tempting out into outdoor areas as they are frightened or overwhelmed by an area that is dominated by active play.

While most outdoor provision works well as discrete areas, flexibility is important. It may be appropriate for some play to flow between areas. For example, in large play areas, play with bikes, scooters and trolleys is enhanced when children have opportunities to make real journeys between interesting places. A wide and winding track for wheeled toys could pass through, for example, a role-play area, a large construction area and wild area. Each stop offers opportunities for social or imaginative interaction. In smaller areas, bike play that spills out into other kinds of play can be intrusive and sometimes dangerous. A more confined and flexible roadway area may be appropriate. Adults can involve children in discussion of roadway design and the need to avoid interrupting other activities by drawing the roadway during the session with playground chalk.

Case study one

Narinder had recently joined Cross Flatts Nursery School and had special responsibility for mathematical and technological learning. After a term, Narinder shared her observations with the team and discussed development work in the outdoor area. As a newcomer, she had observed that mathematical learning was a strength of the setting but was mainly focused indoors. In technology, children worked well with small construction sets, but other activities seemed to be too adult directed, offering few opportunities for children to develop their own ideas. The large and attractive outdoor space could be important in providing a large construction area to strengthen these two aspects of the curriculum.

The team developed plans over a number of months. As they discussed resources, Miriam also shared ideas gained from her reading. She wanted the team to provide open-ended resources, for example blocks, crates, tyres and planks, which would allow children to create their own role-play environments. A wheeled trolley would be particularly useful as it could function as bus, lorry, ambulance or fire engine, depending on the children's elected play theme. Miriam explained how social interaction and language use improves when children use open-ended materials and have to negotiate meanings. The team were encouraged that Miriam and Narinder's ideas seemed to mesh so well.

Figure 1 shows the team's long-term planning for the large construction area. It uses the framework of the English curriculum guidance (DfES/QCA, 2000) but incorporates aspects of thinking about learning dispositions from *Te Whariki* (Ministry of Education, 1996).

Playing Outdoors in the Early Years

Figure 1: Long-term planning for the large construction area

What will the children learn?

Skills
- designing and constructing
- planning
- predicting
- identifying problems/problem-solving
- evaluating
- comparing
- marching and sorting
- counting
- sharing and co-operating
- communicating
- negotiating
- asking questions
- imaging
- taking on a role
- climbing, jumping and balancing
- reading and mark-making

Learning dispositions
- taking an interest
- being involved
- persisting with challenge and difficulty
- expressing an idea/feeling point of view
- taking responsibility

Knowledge and understanding of
- materials, e.g. wood, plastic, rubber and net
- balance and symmetry
- shape and space
- measurement
- size
- transportation
- position, e.g. on, off, under and behind
- connection
- horizontality and verticality
- grids
- enclosure and envelopment
- adult roles
- print

Key learning goals

Knowledge and understanding of the world
- ask questions about why things happen and how things work
- build and construct with a wide range of objects, selecting appropriate resources and adapting their work where necessary
- investigate objects and materials by using all of their senses as appropriate

Physical development
- show awareness of space, of themselves and of others
- use a range of small and large equipment

Mathematical development
- use developing mathematical ideas and methods to solve practical problems

- use language such as 'circle' or 'bigger' to describe the shape and size of solids and flat shapes
- use everyday words to describe position

Creative development
- explore colour, texture, shape, form and space in two or three dimensions
- use their imagination in role-play
- express and communicate their ideas, thoughts and feelings through role play

Resources
- hollow blocks
- crates, tyres, cones, ropes
- trolley
- toolset, measuring tape
- mark-making box
- Book box with fiction and non-fiction books
- Laminated song and rhyme sheets
- Album of photos of children's work
- Box of fabric
- Pegs

The adult role

- make continuous provision with regular adult observation and interaction
- encourage children to experiment with the materials
- introduce appropriate vocabulary and questions to extend children's thinking
- take on a play-tutoring role with inexperienced children
- provide supplementary resources in labelled baskets
- take digital photographs of children working
- introduce laminated sheets of photos and albums as a stimulus for ideas
- introduce props in response to children's ideas and play themes
- introduce 'girl day' sessions if the area is dominated by boys

---

Evaluating long-term plans

It is important for teams to evaluate planning for outdoor learning. The evaluation of long-term plans is considered in detail here. Practitioners will need to give similar consideration to the evaluation of medium- and short-term plans.

Playing Outdoors in the Early Years

Long-term plans for key areas of outdoor provision can be reviewed over time, perhaps focusing on an area every six weeks. When monitoring an area, it is useful to ask general questions about how the area is working, for example:

- Which children work in the area?

- How regularly do children return to the area?

- What is the approximate length of time children stay in the area?

- What do children do and say in the area?

- What are children learning in the area?

An observation record (Figure 2) can support practitioners in undertaking regular but brief observations.

As practitioners evaluate areas, they can draw on their observation to ask questions and make judgements about the effectiveness of the outdoor provision.

For example, practitioners evaluating the outdoor construction area might ask:

- Do girls and boys regularly become involved in designing and building?

- Are children identifying problems and finding solutions to problems?

- Are children using mathematical language to talk about shape and space?

Judgements made can inform decisions about necessary changes to enhance the opportunities for learning outdoors. The observation record also provides ideas for supporting the learning of groups and individuals who are working at very different levels.

Figure 2: An observation record

Area of provision: large construction		Date: September 2003
Children	Activity, language and learning	Next Steps
Amrit, Davinder and Megan	• Worked co-operatively, building a princess castle enclosure made with crates and with cones placed on top. • Amrit: 'Let's make our bed now and the princesses are tired.' (time: approximately one hour)	• Introduce books about castles, note architecture such as turrets. • Suggest drawing plans of castles.
Connor	• Working alone, loads crates onto trolley and transports them across the playground. Tips crates into a pile. 'I've got leads of bricks.' (time: 10 minutes)	• Encourage and support play with play partner. • Look at photos of simple constructions.
Mohammed and Jack	• Placed crates in a horizontal line and added tyres vertically. • 'We're friends, right.' 'Yeah, mate.'	• Provide a commentary on actions such as, 'That crate's going next to that one. You're making a line now.'

An additional approach to evaluation of the outdoor curriculum involves monitoring across areas of provision. Here the focus of monitoring could be on the opportunities for learning within a specific curriculum area, for example ICT. Alternatively, the focus could be an aspect of the curriculum such as cultural diversity. Case study two provides an example of monitoring a curriculum area.

Case study two

The staff at Hillcrest Early Years Centre had recently attended in-service training focused on ICT. They were particularly interested in approaches used in UK, Portuguese and Swedish settings (Siraj-Blatchford and Siraj-Blatchford 2003), where ICT had been integrated into aspects of play-based provision. All agreed on the value of increasing children's awareness of the uses of ICT in everyday contexts, to promote positive dispositions towards learning about and through ICT. It was decided that development work would start with an audit of provision indoors and outdoors, followed by a listing of possible developments (Figure 3). Although aware that ICT might not link to all areas of provision, they decided to consider each area in turn.

Medium-term planning for outdoor learning

Areas of outdoor play provision, available continuously or near continuously, provide the

Planning an Outdoor Curriculum

Figure 3: Outdoor ICT audit

Outdoor provision	Existing ICT provision	Possible ICT provision
• wet and dry sand		*
• painting area		*
• water area		*
• digging areas		*
• large construction		• mobile phones • programmable toy vehicles
• small construction		
• mark-making area		
• music area		• battery-operated children's tape-recorder for music
• garden area		*
• wild area		*
• physical area		
• role-play area	• telephone box • toy microwave	• mobile phones • electric till for shop • walkie-talkies (police and fire-fighter role-play)
• roadway	• traffic lights	• mobile phones • electronic till for garage • programmable toy vehicles
• book area		• album of outdoor photos taken with digital camera
• general provision		• digital camera
• related indoor provision		• video clips and internet links extending outdoor experiences, such as the life-cycle of the butterfly

main context for children's learning outdoors. However, there are times when medium-term themes or enhancements, planned in response to children's interests and thinking, can enrich opportunities for learning outdoors. These may arise from predictable and interesting events, for example a cold spell of wintry weather that promises frost, ice and possibly snow. They can also be developed from children's observed interests. Children's preoccupation with the schemas of going through and enveloping (Athey, 1990), for example, can provide a useful starting point for building dens or a role-play camp. Favourite stories, such as the *Three Billy Goats Gruff*, also provide valuable starting points for medium-term enhancements of provision.

Some medium-term plans will focus solely on outdoor provision, for example a focus on dens. However, in many cases medium-term planning will offer links between indoor and outdoor learning. For example, children's fascination with the first spring bulbs in the garden can be supported and extended through creative work, using a variety of art media, both indoors and outdoors.

When planning themes and enhancements, the duration should be flexible and responsive to children's interests. However, it is important to note the importance of repetition for young children's learning. This is evidenced by children's repeated requests for favourite stories, songs and rhymes. Elliot (1999) suggests that repeated experiences are not only enjoyable but help to reinforce valuable neural pathways in the brain. To ensure that outdoor environments offer opportunities for repeated experience and allow children to consolidate and extend learning, it is important that key activities and experiences are offered over time (Edgington, 1998). Children, for example, may enjoy the novelty of a role-play garage for a week, but they are likely to gain more from involvement in the development of a play theme over a more extended period.

Case study three

Lian and Jim worked in the Karinga Infant School reception class. They had noticed that two favourite picture books were stories about young children playing outdoors. One of these, *Sally's Secret* (Shirley Hughes, 1992) centred on a girl of about four, who loved finding places to hide. She made houses in all sorts of secret places, both alone and with her best friend. Lian and Jim felt that this story, with its bird, ladybird and cat each welcomed as visitors into the girls' secret house, captured the reception children's delight in being outdoors, close to the natural world. Another favourite story, *Whistle for Willie* (Ezra Jack Keats, 1964) was set in the contrasting urban landscape of a US city. In this story, Peter also enjoyed finding places to hide and playing at grown-ups, in this case accompanied by his dog Willie.

The two books were used by Lian and Jim to stimulate talk about what the reception children liked most outdoors. Dens, animals and playing with friends were high on the list. This seemed to be a great starting point for a summer-time enhancement of the reception garden. Thinking through their plans, Lian and Jim were particularly pleased to have a theme that would support a focus on friendship. Two new children had recently joined the class and, one of them, Carly, was having difficulties settling into the group. Lian and Jim felt that the planned activities would provide a good context for supporting integration of the new children.

Following discussions, Lian and Jim drew up a medium-term plan (Figure 4), drawing on the Experiential Education curriculum framework (Laevers, 2000).

At the end of this successful focus, Lian and Jim evaluated their planning and the work undertaken to inform future practice. They asked questions relating to the following aspects:

- timing
- manageability
- the balance of child-initiated and adult-directed work
- match to children's interests
- match to children's developmental levels
- quality and range of resources
- involvement of parents/carers
- evidence of children's learning

Planning an Outdoor Curriculum

Figure 4: Karinga reception class: medium-term planning

Focus of interest/theme: outdoor play stories, songs and rhymes

---

Date: June 2003   Expected duration: 4 weeks

Key learning goals
- emotional health
- curiosity and the exploratory drive
- expression and communication skills
- imagination and creativity
- the competence of self-organization
- understanding the world of objects and people

Focus activities and experiences
- listen to and discuss stories and rhymes about outdoor play
- talk about special friends and making sure that everyone has a play partner
- negotiate and record plans for dens and secret houses
- build and evaluate dens and secret houses, using a variety of materials
- explore the properties of materials to keep out the sun on hot days and keep out the rain on wet days
- use language to create roles and stories while playing in dens and secret houses
- search for and closely observe animals in the garden, e.g. birds, spiders, ladybirds, beetles, worms and butterflies

- use books, video clips and the internet to find out more about the animals observed
- record observations of animals through drawing, painting, collage and clay work

Resources
- wild area
- crates, blocks and logs
- folding clothes-dryer
- quadro frames
- variety of fabrics, e.g. net, cotton, muslin, plastic and wool
- variety of joining materials, e.g. pegs, bulldog clips, string and masking tape
- role-play props, e.g. tea-set, dolls and soft animals
- natural materials for role-play, e.g. pine cones, pebbles and shells
- laminated song and rhyme sheets, e.g. Ladybird, ladybird fly away home
- outdoor stories, e.g. *Sally's Secret*, *Whistle for Willie*
- magnifiers
- reference books about birds and mini-beasts
- art boards for outdoor drawing, e.g. pencils, charcoal and pastels

Playing Outdoors in the Early Years

Focus of interest/theme: outdoor play stories, songs and rhymes	
Date: June 2003	Expected duration: 4 weeks

- indoor art area, computers and videos

Appropriate questions (present, future, past)
- What materials will you need?
- How will you join the materials?
- How will you make it strong?
- Which material do you think will keep out the hot sun/wet rain?
- What do you think will happen if …?
- Was it a good house? In what ways? How could you have made it better?
- What can you see if you look very closely? What is it doing?

Appropriate vocabulary
- large, small, shape, space, straight, tall, long, wide, high, narrow

- join, connect, fasten
- strong, weak
- warm, cool, wet, dry, waterproof, shade
- net, cotton, muslin, plastic, wool, card, foil, wood
- pine cones, pebbles, shells, soil, grass
- bird names, spider, ladybird, beetle, ant, worm, caterpillar, butterfly, centipede
- soft, smooth, slippery, furry, spiky, prickly, shiny

Involvement of parents/carers
- send song and rhyme sheets home
- send home tally sheet for children to record animals seen at home in a day
- invite parent/family helpers to support the work

Short-term planning for outdoor learning

Early years settings are complex organizations and may include children with diverse needs. Usually there is a wide range of activities on offer and there will be at least two adults in the staff team. A variety of other adults may be present, including parents, carers, students and other professionals. In complex settings of this kind, short-term planning is the key to ensuring that long- and medium-term plans for the outdoor area are effectively realized. Short-term planning provides a framework for focused teaching with individuals, as well as small and large groups. It can be used to ensure an appropriate balance in the adult support provided for adult-initiated and child-initiated play and activities (DfES/QCA, 2000).

Case study four

At the Bennett Street Pre-school weekly staff meeting, Di and Woan Chan shared their recent observations of children's learning in the outdoor area. Both were concerned that the current staff rota, moving adults between areas several times a day, was contributing to superficial levels of adult engagement with play. This seemed to be particularly problematic outdoors, where some staff took on a primarily supervisory role. Although children played happily outside, conflicts were relatively common and more complex play unusual. Both practitioners felt frustrated by a lack of opportunity to tackle these problems in a sustained way, and proposed a change to the staffing schedule to allow staff to focus on each area for a week. They hoped that this would support higher levels of engagement by both children and staff. Some staff opposed the change, primarily because weather conditions sometimes made the outdoor supervisory role difficult. However, with agreement to allow for flexibility in poor weather,

---

the team decided to trial this new approach. The new weekly planning grid, with indoor and outdoor focus activities, is shown in Figure 5. .

Figure 5: Weekly rota and focus activities

Rota for week beginning: 18 October 2003

		Monday	Tuesday	Wednesday	Thursday	Friday
Outside	Di	Obstacle course —————————————————→ Planting bulbs ————→
Carpeted area	Emma	Storytelling focus ————————————————————————————————→
Tiled wet area	Nick	Colour-mixing focus ——————————————————————————————→
Flexible staff	Woan Chan	——————————————————————————→
	Rona (student)	——→

The Bennett Street team agreed to retain other effective aspects of their short-term planning. Their observation and assessment focus worked well and this, along with evaluations of focus activities, was important in feeding back into future planning. They also liked having three adults responsible for areas, while the fourth and any additional adults were used more flexibly. This flexibility was particularly important when large numbers of children chose to play outside. It also meant that an adult was available to provide support when someone was leading an activity such as planting bulbs. The team was particularly keen to retain a balance of adult time between focus activities, developed from long- and medium-term plans, and engagement with the spontaneous child-led events of the day.

The Bennett Street team had agreed to focus regularly on physical play. They wanted all children to enjoy active, physical play, and they aimed to provide appropriate levels of challenge for physically confident children. This week's outdoor planning for an obstacle course was drawn from long-term plans for the physical area (Figure 6). The second outdoor plan was for a focus on planting bulbs, drawn from medium-term planning for an autumn theme.

At the end of the week, the weather changed from warm and sunny to persistent rain. The ground was muddy and it was not good weather for planting bulbs. However, the team had in place some flexible planning for a rainy day,

Playing Outdoors in the Early Years

supported by a range of resources stored in boxes. These included spare wellies and waterproof clothes; a variety of umbrellas;

Figure 6: Bennett Street Pre-school: short-term planning

Adult: Di

Focus area: physical development Activity area/s, outdoor physical area

Learning goals	*Monitoring and assessment*
• to explore movement, to travel around, under, over and through large apparatus • to use language to talk about actions	• observe children's levels of confidence, motivation to explore movement and use of language to talk about actions

---

Grouping: friendship groups of up to six

Individual needs
- extension – explore and describe new ways of moving
- new children learning English as an additional language – focus on highlighted vocabulary
- encourage participation with adult support – Maria, Sian, Kiranjit, Jamie

Activity
- children help to set up the obstacle course, explaining how the apparatus could be used
- free movement around the circuit

Resources
- hollow blocks and planks, hurdles, flexible and rigid tunnels, plastic steps, hoops and rope

Key questions
- Questions about the present, e.g. What are you doing? Which part is touching the bench?
- Questions about the future, e.g. How could you do it differently next time?
- Questions about the past, e.g. Can you remember how you first moved through the tunnel … and then how you did it?

Key vocabulary
- provide a commentary on actions, e.g. You are high up
- names of apparatus, body parts, high, low, around, under, over, through, on, top, slow, fast, slide, pull, crawl, wriggle, stretch, jump

containers, pipes and guttering for collecting, measuring and moving water; as well as several storybooks and laminated cards with songs and rhymes about rainy weather. Despite some short bursts of heavy rain, Di was able to work effectively outdoors through the week, with groups of children enthusiastic to play out in the rain or to watch with fascination from the shelter of a small play-house.

The adult role

Consideration of the adult role is a key aspect of planning for outdoor play and important at each level of planning. The adult role as educator is far more concerned with interaction than the primarily supervisory role of adults during school play-times or lunch periods. Perry's (2001) case study of an American nursery school suggests that, although skilled practitioners will often leave children to play independently, this should arise from a careful judgment about how, when or if to intervene, based on detailed observations of individuals and groups.

Research suggests a key role for adults in supporting young children's learning, particularly through language (Nind, 2001; Siraj-Blatchford *et al.*, 2002). Nind, who led an action-research study focused on language development in the early years unit of a London primary school, identifies a special role for outdoor play as an effective context for children's talk. These studies suggest the need for adults to adopt an informal, conversational-style outdoors, following the lead of children's play and talk. It seems that more controlling and managerial adult styles place unintended blocks on opportunities for learning through language. Siraj-Blatchford, *et al.* (2002, p. 10) suggest that the most effective adult–child interactions take place over longer periods than more typically brief adult–child exchanges and incorporate elements of 'sustained shared thinking'.

Adults have a key role as conversational partners during outdoor play. The role of play tutor (Aubrey *et al.*, 2000), where the adult joins in play to provide a model and to suggest or extend play ideas, is also an important one. This is particularly important where adults are working with children who are inexperienced players.

Well-planned outdoor learning environments provide rich opportunities for learning but raise some specific planning issues. This section has presented a flexible approach to planning that includes positive strategies to support learning and teaching outdoors, while taking account of some key issues.

In the earlier discussion of curriculum frameworks, reference was made to the ways that purposes and goals are shaped by diverse cultures and vary across curriculum frameworks (Spodek and Saracho, 1996). The section that follows provides some contrasting and successful examples of approaches to planning an outdoor curriculum, shaped by very different cultural contexts.

6

Outdoor Learning in Early Years Curricula Internationally

> *Each culture identifies the content of its education in relation to the knowledge it values, not just for personal growth, but because it reflects the society's view of what is true, what is right, what is beautiful.*
>
> (Spodek and Saracho, 1996, p. 11)

Outdoor play and learning is identified as an important strand of the early childhood curriculum in many countries. However, there are differences in approach and emphasis that reflect the contrasting values of different countries, shaped by 'cultural, economic, political and historic factors' (Ofsted, 2003, p. 43). While it is not possible or appropriate to replicate in detail practice from very different cultural contexts, it is valuable to look to the ideas informing practice in other countries (Spodek and Saracho, 1996; Ofsted, 2003). This section presents three very different examples of successful outdoor learning from the contrasting cultural contexts of northern Italy, England and Norway.

The Villetta pre-school in Reggio Emilia

The first pre-school of Reggio Emilia, in north Italy, was founded on Liberation Day, 1945 at the end of the war. The community of this town came together to build a pre-school from the rubble of destroyed buildings, creating a symbol of promise for a better future. Growing out of these special circumstances and following the defeat of fascism in Italy, the Reggio Emilia schools developed a unique philosophy. This distinctive approach, emphasizing the child as confident and competent, and rich in potential, was developed by Loris Malaguzzi in collaboration with early years educators, parents and the community. It has inspired interest internationally.

One important strand within the Reggio Emilia philosophy is the emphasis on the physical environment and resources for children's learning (Dudek, 2000). The environment, in interaction with children and resources, is seen as 'the third teacher'; it includes both the nursery garden and the wider environment of the town. Another important strand is the social-constructivist philosophy – children are encouraged to develop their thinking in the supportive social contexts provided by peers and teachers. One special outdoor project undertaken by three- to six-year-olds at Villetta pre-school, 'the amusement park for birds' (Reggio Children, 1995), provides a fascinating example of these strands in practice.

Five- and six-year-olds initiated the idea for the project during a series of extensive class discussions around the needs of the birds that inhabited the school grounds. Having settled on the exciting idea of creating an amusement park for the birds, the children set out on their co-operative project. One of the children's important ideas was to provide fountains for the birds. The research began with two field trips where children observed, talked about, drew and photographed the beautiful fountains of their city. Following extensive discussion and drawing activity back in the pre-school, the children made clay models of fountains, painted them, and engaged in extended theorizing about the workings of the fountains. Finally, with the support of their teachers, the children were ready to experiment with water, pipes, tanks, sprays, water wheels and a variety of other materials to create model fountains. Following an extended period of exploratory work, a variety of complex and beautiful fountains were constructed in the garden of the school, set out as an amusement park for the birds, and opened with a special community celebration.

It is the process of, firstly, developing ideas as a group and, secondly, communicating these through a range of languages that are two of the most important aspects of this outdoor project. As they work together through the different stages of the project, these children are developing a rich repertoire of 'logical, co-operative, expressive, imaginative and symbolic' languages (Reggio Children, 1995, p. 16).

Images of the distinctive Reggio Emilia pre-schools and examples of the children's creative work can be found at: *www.zerosei.comune.re.it/ inter/nidiescuole.htm*.

Forest Schools in Norway

From the very different culture of the Scandinavian countries, forest schools represent a further tradition

Playing Outdoors in the Early Years

with relevance for early childhood education. Currently, the ideals of the Forest School movement are having a growing impact on thinking about an outdoor curriculum for young children (Grenier, 1999).

Forest schools represent a significant strand of early childhood education in Norway, where physical education has a high status and there is a strong and shared belief that young children should experience an active and outdoor childhood. The geography and climate of Norway must contribute to the high value placed on educating children as confident and skilful citizens in outdoor environments. A high proportion of the Norwegian children who attend early childhood settings up to six years of age are offered extended periods of outdoor activities, active play and exercise. Many of these children gain experience of play and exercise within physically challenging environments and through all seasons of the year (OECD, 1999).

Recent research in a Norwegian pre-school (Fjortoft, 2001) suggests that challenging physical experiences can impact on the physical fitness of young children in positive ways. Fjortoft (2001) undertook quasi-experimental research with groups of five- to seven-year-olds from three kindergartens. One group enjoyed a wide variety of physical and creative play experiences and activities for one to two hours a day in a forest play-scape, situated at the edge of the kindergarten. The forest area included slopes, cliffs, rocks, plains and woodland vegetation. Children could play independently in the area closest to the kindergarten. They were also accompanied by adults on regular visits further into the forest. In the other two kindergartens, children enjoyed similar periods of outdoor play, but in traditional outdoor play areas with standard playground equipment. Over the year of the study, children in the experimental group showed gradually improved motor ability, particularly in relation to balance and co-ordination. It seems that the natural landscape, compared with a traditional and well-equipped playground, increased opportunities for physical development.

Children who explored the more challenging forest play-scape may have made further gains in their personal and emotional development. However, this was not documented in the Norwegian study. Concern for the social and emotional dimension of young children's experience has been particularly influential in the development of practice in forest schools within the UK. At the forest school at Bridgewater Early Excellence Centre, children who lack confidence or who have behavioural difficulties, particularly seem to benefit from their forest experiences (Grenier, 1999). It seems that the distinctive practice of the Scandinavian forest schools has relevance for practitioners working in very different cultural contexts. Images and an account of the work of the forest school movement in Oxfordshire, England can be found at: *www.news.bbc.co.uk/1/hi/education/2957379.stm.*

Growing Schools in England

The Growing Schools initiative in the UK represents another important strand of outdoor education. The tradition of growing vegetables and flowers with young children reaches back into the first half of the 19th century with the educational work of Froebel. Funded by the UK government, Growing Schools set out to encourage schools for all age groups to make better use of outdoor environments for teaching and learning. Specific aims of the initiative include to increase children's awareness and understanding of farming and growing; to increase opportunities for first-hand experience; and to increase children's understanding of, and responsibility for, the environment (DfES, 2002).

A Growing Schools garden was set up at the Hampton Court Flower Show in 2002 to provide an inspiring model of a school garden, with contributions from schools, including several early childhood settings. The contributions demonstrate how a small and barren playground can be transformed into stimulating outdoor classroom, with imaginative and innovative ideas but with a minimum of expenditure. Young children and children with special educational needs were actively involved in the creation of the different elements of an inspiring garden. These included herbs and vegetables grown in decorated and recycled containers; bird feeders and nest boxes; decorated pots and pans for a musical washing line; and a multi-sensory interactive pergola. The Growing Schools initiative demonstrates how children's active participation in planning, designing and making a garden is essential if they are to develop a real sense of responsibility for the environment. It suggests that an educational garden should be designed as an evolving environment, with each new cohort of children contributing new ideas.

The Coombes Infants and Nursery School in Reading was one of the schools that participated in this garden project and its environmental work, which is at the centre of the school curriculum, exemplifies this approach. Every child is involved throughout the year in the cycle of planting, growing and harvesting, for example, contributing to the school sunflower garden. Children are also involved in celebrating many festivals and these often link to their work in the garden and wildlife areas. The outdoor environment is used in imaginative ways to engage children in significant experience. For example, at the millennium, children, the staff and their families joined together for a night-time outdoor celebration which involved the lighting of 2000 candles. The Coombes Infants and Nursery School demonstrates a meaningful link with the philosophy and practice of Froebel in the way that it offers young children significant experiences in the outdoor environment, experiences that nurture a sense of both community and spirituality. Images of active outdoor education at The Coombes Infants and Nursery School can be found at: *www.thecoombes.com/frames.html.*

7

Sources of Advice, Guidance and Support

This book has presented many examples of practitioners who successfully nourish young children's learning in outdoor environments. High-quality practice can be found across a wide range of settings and in very different communities; it can be found in inner-city schools providing rich play environments in the smallest of yards, as well as kindergartens set on the edge of the forest.

Creating outdoor environments for play and learning is challenging but rewarding. It takes time, and should be planned as a long-term project that evolves through a number of phases. A wide range of knowledge and skills underpin successful development work, and there are significant benefits in involving children, colleagues and families in the process. Additionally, a number of organizations, local and national, provide valuable advice, guidance and support. Some starting points are listed below.

Consulting with children

◆ Save the Children is an international organization that is concerned with children's rights and has particular expertise in consulting with children. Details of a number of relevant publications can be accessed at: *www.savethechildren.org.uk.*

Sources of Advice, Guidance and Support

Developing the outdoor environment

- Learning through Landscapes is a UK charity that undertakes research, gives advice and encourages action to improve school grounds as environments for learning. Details of its work and publications can be found at: *www.ltl.org.uk.*
- Groundwork is a UK environmental regeneration charity. It supports environmental development work, particularly in the UK's poorest communities. Details about its work can be accessed at: *www.groundwork.org.uk.*
- British Trust for Conservation Volunteers is a UK charity that works with people to bring about positive environmental change. It offers guidance and practical support to develop wildlife areas in the grounds of schools and other early years settings. Information about the charity can be accessed at: *www.btcv.org.*
- Evergreen is a Canadian charity and environmental organization that has a mandate to bring nature to the city through naturalization projects. Information about its work, including work in school grounds, can be accessed at: *www.evergreen.ca.*
- American Community Gardening Association a national non-profit membership organization of professionals, volunteers and supporters of community greening in urban and rural communities. It supports a number of projects in educational settings. Details of its work can be accessed at: *www.communitygarden.org/index.html.*

Playing Outdoors in the Early Years

- The Natural Learning Initiative is an American organization, based at North Carolina State University. It aims to promote the importance of the natural environment in children's daily experience through environmental design, action research, education and dissemination of information. Details of this work can be accessed at: *www.naturalearning.org*.
- The Edible Schoolyard is a non-profit program, focused on a kitchen garden that is located on the campus of Martin Luther King Junior Middle School in Berkley, California. The program website provides a number of useful links. It can be accessed at: *www.edibleschoolyard.org/about.html*.

Developing inclusive outdoor environments

- Sensory Trust is a UK charity that offers consultancy and advice on inclusive designs for outdoor environments. Information about the organization and its publications can be accessed at: *www.sensorytrust.org.uk*.
- Let's Play Projects is a US organization that provides support to promote playfulness in young children with disabilities, as well as information about accessible materials. There are useful links within the site. It can be accessed at: *www.cosmos.ot.buffalo.edu/letsplay/ index.html*.

References

Anning, A. (1997), *The First Years at School*. Buckingham: Open University Press.

Athey, C. (1990), *Extending Thought in Young Children: A Parent-teacher partnership*. London: Paul Chapman.

Aubrey, C., David, T., Godfrey, R. and Thomas, L. (2000), *Early Childhood Educational Research*. London: RoutledgeFalmer.

Baldock, P. (2001), *Regulating Early Years Services*. London: David Fulton.

Bilton, H. (2002), *Outdoor Play in the Early Years: Management and innovation* second edition. London: David Fulton.

Bishop, J. (2001), 'Creating places for living and learning' in L. Abbott and C. Nutbrown (eds), *Experiencing Reggio Emilia Implications for Pre-school Provision*. Buckingham and Philadelphia: Open University Press, pp. 72–9.

Bradford Education (1995), *'Can I play out?' Outdoor Play in the Early Years*. Bradford: Bradford Education.

Bredecamp, S. (ed) (1987), *Developmentally Appropriate Practice in Early Childhood Programs Serving Children from Birth Through Age 8*. Washington: National Association for the Education of Young Children.

Bruce, T. (1997), *Early Childhood Education*. London: Hodder and Stoughton.

Charlton, M. (2002), 'Sharing good practice: animal welfare. Hop to it!' *Nursery World*, 30 May 2002.

Clark, A. and Moss, P. (2001), *Listening to Young Children: The mosaic approach*. London: National Children's Bureau.

Connolly, P. (1998), *Racism, Gender Identities and Young Children*. London: Routledge.

Corsaro, W. (1997), *The Sociology of Childhood*. California: Pine Forge.

Dahlberg, G., Moss, P. and Pence, A. (eds) (1999), *Beyond Quality in Early Childhood Education and Care*. London: Falmer.

De Hann, D. and Singer, E. (2001), 'Young children's language of togetherness' in *International Journal of Early Years Education*. 9, (2), pp. 117–24.

DfEE (1990), *Starting with quality: The report of the committee of enquiry into the quality of educational experience offered to 3- and 4-year-olds*. London: HMSO.

DfEE/QCA (2000), *Curriculum Guidance for the Foundation Stage*. London: QCA.

DfES (2002), *Growing Schools*. London: DfES.

Doctoroff, S. (2001), 'Adapting the physical environment to meet the needs of all young children for play' in *Early Childhood Education Journal*. 29, (2), pp. 105–9.

Drake, J. (2001), *Planning Children's Play and Learning in the Foundation Stage*. London: David Fulton.

Drummond, M. (2000), 'Comparisons in early years education' (online) in *Early Childhood Research and Practice*. 2, (1). Last accessed on 10 February 2003 at: *www.ecrp.uiuc.edu/v2n1/drummond.html*.

Dudek, M. (2000), *Kindergarten Architecture: Space for the Imagination* (second edition). London: Spon Press.

Early Childhood Mathematics Group (2001), 'Foundation stage mathematics' in *Mathematics Teaching*. 175, pp. 20–2.

Edgington, M. (1998), *The Nursery Teacher in Action* (second edition). London: Paul Chapman.

Edgington, M. (2002), *The Great Outdoors*. London: Early Education.

Elliot, L. (1999), *Early Intelligence: How the Brain and Mind Develop in the First Five Years of Life*. London: Penguin.

Ellis, N. (2002), *Firm Foundations? A Survey of ATL Members Working in the Foundation Stage*. London: Association of Teachers and Lecturers.

Fjortoft, (2001) 'The natural environment as a playground for children: the impact of outdoor play activities in pre-primary school children' in *Early Childhood Education Journal*. 29 (2), pp. 11–117.

Gallahue, D. L. and Ozmun, J. (1998), *Understanding Motor Development* (fourth edition). Dubuque, Iowa: McGraw-Hill.

Grenier, J. (1999), 'The Great Outdoors' in *Nursery World*. 16 September 1999.

Harms, T., Clifford, R. and Cryer, D. (1998), *Early Childhood Environment Rating Scale Revised Edition*. New York and London: Teachers College Press.

Hart, R. (1979), *Children's Experience of Place*. New York: Irvington Publishers.

Henry, J. (2003), 'Ministers launch new assault on gender gap' in *Times Educational Supplement*. 17 January 2003, p. 16.

Hestenes, L. and Carroll, D. (2000), 'The play inter-actions of young children with and without disabilities: individual and environmental influences' in *Early Childhood Research Quarterly*. 15, (2), pp. 229–46.

Hetherington, S. (2001), 'Kindergarten: garden pedagogy from romanticism to reform' in *Landscape Journal*. 20, (1), pp. 30–4.

Hood, S. (2001), *The State of London's Children*. London: Office of the Children's Rights Commissioner for London.

Hughes, S. (1992), *Sally's Secret*. London: Red Fox.

Isaacs, S. (1932), *The Nursery Years: The mind of the child from birth to six years*. Routledge and Kegan Paul.

James, A., Jenks C. and Prout, A. (1999), *Theorising Childhood*. Cambridge: Polity Press.

Keats, Ezra Jack, (1964), *Whistle for Willie*. London: Bodley Head.

Laevers, F. (2000), 'Forward to basics! Deep-level-learning and the experiential approach' in *Early Years*. 20, (2), pp. 20–9.

Learning through Landscapes (2003), *10 Years of Learning through Landscapes*. Winchester: Learning Through Landscapes.

Liebschner, J. (2001), *A Child's Work Freedom and Guidance in Froebel's Educational Theory and Practice*. Cambridge: The Lutterworth Press.

McNaughton, G. (1992), 'Equity Challenges for the Early Childhood Curriculum' in *Children and Society*. *6*, (3), pp. 325–40.

McNaughton, G. and Williams, G. (1998), *Techniques for Teaching Young Children*. Melbourne: Addison Wesley Longman.

Meadows, S. (1993), *The Child as Thinker*. London and New York: Routledge.

Miller, K. (1989), *The Outside Play and Learning Book*. Maryland: Gryphon House.

Millward, A. and Whey, R. (1997), *Facilitating Play on Housing Estates*. London: Chartered Institute of Housing and Joseph Rowntree Foundation.

Moore, R. (1985), *Childhood's Domain: play and place in child development*. Croom Helm.

Nabhan (1994a), 'A child's sense of wildness', in G. Nabhan and S. Trimble (eds) *The Geography of Childhood. Why Children Need Wild Places*. Boston: Beacon Press, pp. 3–14.

Nabhan (1994b), 'Children in touch, creatures in story', in G. Nabhan and S. Trimble (eds) *The Geography of Childhood: why children need wild places*. Boston: Beacon Press, pp. 77–107.

Nind, M. (2001), 'Enhancing the communication learning environment of an early years unit' in *Education-Line* (online). Last accessed 7 January 2003 at: *www.leeds.ac.uk/educol/documents/00001920.htm*.

Ofsted (2001), *Nursery Education: Quality of provision for 3 and 4 year olds 2000–2001*. London: Ofsted.

Ofsted (2003), *The Education of Six Year Olds in England, Denmark and Finland*. London: Ofsted.

Organization for Economic Co-operation and Development (1999), *OECD Country Note Early Childhood Education and Care Policy in Norway* (online). Last accessed 25 February 2003 at: *www.oecd.org/pdf/M00020000/M0020292.pdf*.

Ouvry, M. (2000), *Excercising Muscles and Minds:*

Outdoor play and the early years curriculum. London: The National Early Years Network.

Pascal, C. and Bertram, T. (1997), *Effective Early Learning: Case studies in improvement.* London: Hodder and Stoughton.

Pellegrini, A. D. and Smith, P. K. (1998), 'Physical activity play: The nature and function of a neglected aspect of play' in *Child Development,* 69, (3), pp. 577–98.

Perry, J. (2001), *Outdoor Play: Teaching strategies with young children.* New York: Teachers College Press.

Raban, B., Ure, C. and Waniganayake, M. (2003), 'Multiple perspectives: acknowledging the virtue of complexity in measuring quality' in *Early Years.* 23, (1), pp. 67–77.

Reggio Children (1995), *Le fontane. The fountains.* Reggio Emilia: Reggio Children S. r. l.

Robb, M. (2001), 'The changing experience of childhood' in P. Foley, J. Roche and S. Tucker (eds), *Children in Society.* Basingstoke: Palgrave.

Rogers, R. (1999), *Planning an Appropriate Curriculum for the Under Fives.* London: David Fulton.

Salmon, P., Taggart, B., Smees, R., Sylva, K., Melhuish, E., Siraj-Blatchford, I. and Eliot, K. (2003), *The Early Years Transition and Special Educational Needs (EYTSEN) Project.* London: DfES.

Schaffer, H. R. (1996), *Social Development.* Oxford: Blackwell.

Senda, M. (1992), *Design of Children's Play Environments.* New York: McGraw-Hill.

Sharp, C. (1998), 'Age of starting school and the early years curriculum: a select annotated bibliography' in

National Foundation for Educational Research Conference Proceedings, 6 October, 1998. London: National Foundation for Educational Research.

Shell, E. R. (2003), *The Hungry Gene: The science of fat and the future of thin*. New Delhi: Atlantic Books.

Siraj-Blatchford, I., Sylva, K., Muttock, S., Gilden, R. and Bell, D. (2002), *Researching Effective Pedagogy in the Early Years*. London: DfES.

Siraj-Blatchford, J. and Siraj-Blatchford, I. (2003), *Supporting Information and Communication Technology in the Early Years*. Buckingham: Open University Press.

Smith, P. K., Cowie, H. and Blades, M. (2003), *Understanding Children's Development* (fourth edition). Oxford: Blackwell.

Spodek, B and Saracho, O. (1996), 'Culture and the early childhood curriculum' in *Early Child Development and Care*. 123, pp. 1–13.

Steedman, C. (1990), *Childhood, Culture and Class in Britain: Margaret McMillan, 1860–1931*. London: Virago.

Stephenson, A. (2003), 'Physical risk-taking: dangerous or endangered?' in *Early Years*. 23, (1), pp. 35–43.

Stoneham, J. (1996), *Grounds for Sharing*. Godalming: Learning Through Landscapes.

Stoneham, J. (1997), 'Health Benefits'. *Landscape Design*. February 1997, pp. 23–6.

Sylva, K., Roy, C. and Painter, M. (1980), *Childwatching at Playgroup and Nursery School*. London: Grant McIntyre.

Talbot, J. and Frost, J. L. (1989), 'Magical landscapes' in *Childhood Education*. 66, pp. 11–15.

Thomas, N. (2001), 'Listening to children' in P. Foley, J. Roche and S. Tucker (eds), *Children in Society*. Basingstoke: Palgrave.

Titman, W. (1994), *Special Places; Special People: The hidden curriculum of school grounds*. Godalming: World Wildlife Fund UK/Learning Through Landscapes.

Trimble, S. (1994), 'The scripture of maps, the names of trees: A child's landscape' in G. Nabhan and S. Trimble (eds) *The Geography of Childhood: Why children need wild places*. Boston: Beacon Press, pp. 15–31.

Williams, G. M. (1994), 'Talk on the climbing frame', in *Early Child Development and Care*. 102, pp. 81–9.

Wood, E. and Attfield, J. (1996), *Play, Learning and the Early Childhood Curriculum*. London: Paul Chapman.

Woodward, R. J. and Yun, J. (2001), 'The Performance of Fundamental Gross Motor Skills by Children Enrolled in Head Start' in *Early Child Development and Care*. 169, pp. 57–67.